P9-DBT-849

DATE DUE

DEMCO 38-297

THE HIDDEN LINK BETWEEN
Adrenalin
& Stress

Also by Archibald D. Hart, Ph.D.

Feeling Free

Depression: Coping and Caring

Children and Divorce: What to Expect, How to Help

*The Success Factor: Discovering God's Potential
through Reality Thinking*

*Coping with Depression in the Ministry
and Other Helping Professions*

THE HIDDEN LINK BETWEEN

Adrenalin & Stress

THE EXCITING NEW BREAKTHROUGH THAT HELPS YOU OVERCOME STRESS DAMAGE

Dr. Archibald D. Hart

WORD BOOKS
PUBLISHER
WACO, TEXAS

A DIVISION OF
WORD, INCORPORATED

Unless otherwise indicated, Scripture quotations are from the King James Version of the Bible (KJV). Other Scripture quotations are from the following sources: The Living Bible (TLB), copyright 1971 by Tyndale House Publishers, Wheaton, IL, used by permission; the New English Bible (NEB), © The Delegates of The Oxford University Press and the Syndics of The Cambridge University Press, 1961, 1970, reprinted by permission; the New International Version of the Bible (NIV), copyright © 1978 by the New York International Bible Society, used by permission of Zondervan Bible Publishers. *The Jerusalem Bible* (JB), copyright © 1966 by Darton, Longman & Todd, Ltd. and Doubleday and Company, Inc.

Quote found on the part one title page (p. 17) is from Hans Selye, *The Stress of Life* (New York: McGraw-Hill, 1978), p. xv. Quote on the part two title page (p. 65) is also from *The Stress of Life*, pp. 432–433. Quote on the part three title page (p. 129) is from Meyer Friedman and Ray Rosenman, *Type-A Behavior and Your Heart* (New York: Knopf, 1974), p. 167.

Library of Congress Cataloging in Publication Data:
Hart, Archibald D.
    Adrenalin & stress.

    Includes index.
    1. Adrenalin—Physiological effect.   2. Stress
(Psychology)—Prevention.   3. Christian life.
I. Title.   II. Title: Adrenalin and stress.
QP572.A27H37   1985   613   85–22507
ISBN 0-8499-0435-8

Printed in the United States of America

5 6 7 8 9 8   FG   9 8 7 6 5 4 3 2 1

Acknowledgments

To my grandfather, Archibald Daniel Hart, who first taught me how to live a balanced life . . .

To my wife, Kathleen, who continues to teach me how to be a whole person . . .

To my secretary, Susan Nordin, who faithfully and with the spirit of Christ has typed and retyped this manuscript . . .

To my colleagues at Fuller Theological Seminary, who provide personal and professional encouragement . . .

. . . I say thank you.

Contents

List of Figures 9

Preface 11

Part One: Adrenalin Arousal—The Essence
    of Stress Disease 17

    1. Understanding the Nature of Stress 19
    2. How Stress Does Its Damage 32
    3. Stress As "Hurry Sickness" 41
    4. Stress and the Spirit 55

Part Two: Diagnosing Your Adrenalin Arousal 65

    5. Symptoms of Distress 67
    6. Are You an Adrenalin Addict? 83
    7. Adrenalin and Cholesterol 96
    8. Finding the Source of Your Stress 105
    9. How to Monitor Your Adrenalin Arousal 115

Part Three: Healing Your Hurry Sickness 129

    10. Managing Your Adrenalin 131
    11. The Secret of Sleep 149
    12. Learning to Relax 165
    13. Changing Your Type-A Behavior 178
    14. Creativity and Stress 191
    15. Spiritual Antidotes for Stress 207

Appendix 1: Keys to Figures 2, 4, and 5 221

Appendix 2: How to Order Temperature Dots 223

Index 225

List of Figures

1. The Stress Response   36
2. Type-A Behavior Pattern Test   45
3. The Effects of Stress on the Body   74
4. Symptoms of Distress   76
5. Everyday-Hassles Test 108
6. Analyzing Your Stressful Environment 113
7. Using Temperature Dots to Monitor Adrenalin
   Arousal 124

Preface

This book is for hurried people—for normal people who live busy but sometimes hectic lives.

It is for those who strive for excellence in all that they do and who find there isn't enough time in the day to accomplish what they desire.

It is for all those who drive themselves hard and work hard to be the best they can be. (This includes mothers as well as bank managers, and followers as well as leaders.)

It is for those who must be creative and take the initiative to achieve their goals.

In short, this is a book for all those who try to live life to the fullest—in business, ministry, the professions, trades, or school. It is also a book for *me,* because I myself need to heed its message!

Most of us live with a sense of time urgency and a conviction that God wants us to do something meaningful with our lives. Because life is so short and opportunities are limited, many of us hurry through life at a frantic pace, with little tolerance for anything that blocks our goals or delays our accomplishments. While we talk about wanting a closer walk with God and richer human experiences, we devote little time to their pursuit, and we chase ourselves to an early grave by ignoring the effect that "hurry sickness" has on our minds and bodies.

We misunderstand the nature of stress, despite the fact that we have been deluged in recent years with books and magazine articles on the subject. We have more information

about what to eat, whom to avoid, how to exercise, and when
to take vacations than we know what to do with. And no
one would deny that this abundance of advice is helpful—
believe me, it is *very* important.

But what we have not heard clearly enough is that the
essence of stress damage lies not so much in the problems
of life, but in our attitude toward time and the excitement
and pleasure we derive from interesting challenges and demanding schedules. The stress response is a natural form
of arousal. In moderation, it is healthy. But continuous *overarousal* leads to stress disease—and it doesn't matter whether
this is the consequence of overwork, unhappiness, or plain
old-fashioned excitement. Such long-term overarousal and
the excessive flow of those hormones associated with stress
eventually lead to physiological and psychological *distress,*
and the leader among these hormones is *adrenalin.* (See technical note on p. 15.)

Recent research has made it very clear that hyperarousal
of the adrenalin system is the essential causing factor in coronary and artery disease, which is the most serious form of
stress damage. (Of course, cholesterol also plays an important
part. But in the absence of excessive adrenalin recruitment,
cholesterol and many other well-known factors seldom cause
heart disease.)

In addition to coronary and artery disease, many other
kinds and symptoms of stress damage can be traced back
to the excessive flow of adrenalin: headaches (tension and
migraine), gastric problems, ulcers, and high blood pressure.
I believe, therefore, that there is a need for one more book
on the topic of stress, a book designed to help us control
the stress problem at its very fountainhead—our adrenalin
systems.

Can we learn to control our adrenalin production? Can
we so manage our thinking, attitudes, and behavior that we
can reduce the excessive arousal of this hormone and thus
avoid the damaging consequences of living life in high gear?
Can we so live at peace with ourselves and God that we

get out of the tendency to respond to life as if it were one long "emergency"?

The answer is a definite and resounding YES. The techniques I will describe in this book can be summarized by the term, "adrenalin management." The underlying idea is that just as we can learn to control our habits and behaviors, we can also learn to control our tendency to recruit excessive adrenalin and keep it within less destructive limits.

Ever since the late 1930s, when Dr. Hans Selye, the father of stress research, first highlighted the connection between stress and the adrenal hormones in the bodies of animals, there has been a growing conviction among many that the overproduction of adrenalin and related hormones are closely related to stress disease. My own work supports this conviction. For the past twelve years I have worked extensively with stressed patients, developing therapeutic techniques (including those known as "biofeedback") to help people reduce stress symptoms. I have also undertaken a number of research projects in collaboration with my doctoral-level students, looking at the causes and cures for overstress. As a result, I have come to see the adrenalin response as providing a powerful key to unlocking the mystery of stress.

I believe the approach I will take in *Adrenalin & Stress* is unique. It is now becoming accepted that the excessive flow of adrenalin is the essential factor in stress disease, even to the extent that some have suggested the use of medication (such as Inderal) to control its overproduction. To my knowledge, however, no one has yet proposed a method such as this, whereby adrenalin production can be controlled by psychological and spiritual methods.

On the stress management scene recently, a set of techniques called "Type-A Personality Counseling" has emerged. These techniques are similar in intent to what I will propose here, except that they are directed specifically to a limited set of behaviors performed by those individuals who have a "Type-A Personality." "Adrenalin management," as I conceive of it, is important for all of us, no matter what our personality type.

While I don't want to fall into the trap of making unreasonable promises, I believe that if my counsel is faithfully followed, you can significantly reduce your tendency to develop stress disease. And you can reverse to a significant extent the stress damage you already suffer. I know, because not only have I applied these techniques to myself, but I have also used them extensively in my practice as a clinical psychologist specializing in stress management.

For some of you, adrenalin management will mean unlearning an "addiction" to your own adrenalin; you may have become so dependent on the "high" your adrenalin gives you that you have difficulty giving it up. For others, adrenalin management will mean discovering more effective and efficient ways of accomplishing creative tasks than "psyching" yourself up to a high level of arousal. For a few, it will mean learning how to *increase* your adrenalin flow when it is needed in a particular life crisis, because you may tend to be too "hang loose."

For *all* of us, adrenalin management will mean learning how to control our bodies by "holding back" when we want to conserve our energy and "letting go" when an extra "push" is needed.

By learning to balance our adrenalin production, we can achieve maximum energy and freedom to live the life God intends for us. We will be fulfilling the injunction of the apostle Paul who said:

"It is God's will that you should be holy; . . . that each of you should learn to control his [or her] own body in a way that is holy and honorable" (1 Thess. 4:3–4, NIV).

ARCHIBALD D. HART
Pasadena, California

Technical Note

For the sake of simplicity and to avoid being overly technical in this book, I have chosen to use the general term "adrenalin," in some contexts, to describe the many hormones produced by the adrenal glands. The term has a popular connotation that well describes the excitement or arousal that we all experience in response to a threat or challenge. A more technical differentiation of the more than fifty corticosteroids and the catecholamines produced by these glands is not necessary for the purposes of this book. The combined effect of all these hormones is treated as if it were a single event, producing a "fight or flight" response. Interested readers could pursue a more complete understanding of the different roles of these hormones by consulting a textbook on the function of the endocrine glands.

I have also chosen to use the simpler spelling "adrenalin" to refer to the natural hormone produced by the body, although I am aware it is often spelled with an "e" to distinguish it from the commercially manufactured hormone, Adrenalin. Because there is no universal agreement on such usage, I have simply used the spelling which is most comfortable for me.

PART ONE

Adrenalin Arousal—
The Essence
Of Stress Disease

"No one can live without experiencing some degree
of stress. You may think that only serious
disease or intensive physical or mental injury can cause stress.
This is false. Crossing a busy intersection,
exposure to a draft, or even sheer joy
are enough to activate the body's stress mechanism
to some extent. Stress is not even necessarily bad for you;
it is also the spice of life,
for any emotion, any activity, causes stress."
—HANS SELYE
The Stress of Life

"And the peace of God, which passeth all understanding,
shall keep your hearts and minds through Christ Jesus."
—PHILIPPIANS 4:7

1

Understanding
The Nature of Stress

We are entering an extraordinary new age in medicine and the health sciences. On the one hand, we are making remarkable progress in curing illnesses and prolonging life. On the other hand, we are losing the battle against a very simple but elusive problem—*stress.*

Despite medical science's enormous strides in treating illness, the problems that are caused by stress are becoming more prevalent and difficult to treat. The time is rapidly approaching, if it hasn't already arrived, when we will be dying less and less from infectious or invasive disease—but more and more from the ravaging effects of too much stress. And stress disease is different from most forms of illness because we bring it on ourselves!

It's not that we don't know stress is a problem! Our predicament is that we don't really understand the nature of stress or how it does its damage—and therefore we don't know how to prevent that damage. And stress disease, for the most part, *can* be avoided.

At the very core of the stress problem is the Western, twentieth-century lifestyle. The lives of most of us are too hectic and fast-paced. We are driven by a need to succeed, and our hectic lives leave little room for relaxation. It's as if we are trapped on a runaway train and don't know where the brakes are—or the engines of our bodies have jammed at full throttle.

And Christians are not immune from the ravages of stress disease, because being Christian doesn't necessarily mean being free of stress! Sometimes it may mean being under even greater stress, because trying to live a godly life in a godless world can take its toll. But having the right balance of values and priorities can be an important protection against the damage caused by stress. In this book, I hope to be able to show some ways to achieve such a balance.

What Is Stress, Anyway?

The word *stress* means different things to different people. It is a multifaceted response that includes changes in perception, emotions, behavior, and physical functioning. Some think of it only as tension, others as anxiety. Some think of it as good, others as bad. The truth is that we all need a certain amount of stress to keep us alive, although too much of it becomes harmful to us. (When most of us use the term, *stress,* we usually are referring to this harmful aspect—*overstress.* In this book, I will try to distinguish these terms.)

Let's look at some examples that will help us better understand the true nature of stress:

- You only have ten minutes to get to church because you've overslept, and it usually takes you at least twenty! They are counting on you to usher this morning, so you really need to be there on time. And to make matters worse, you can't find your wallet and car keys. You search frantically, losing precious seconds as you become more upset about being late. You become impatient, then angry. *You* are under *STRESS.*
- You have been thinking of going back to school to finish your degree, but it has been a long time since you've been in a classroom. You're not sure whether you can handle schoolwork on top of your other responsibilities. At the same time, you feel the need for some kind of change in your life. So you stew about the situation, unable to make a decision. *You* are under *STRESS.*
- As you drive to an appointment, the freeway is more

crowded than usual. You decide to move to another lane, only to find that it is even slower than the one you were in. You become irritated and mumble a few words under your breath at the driver in front of you. *You* are under *STRESS.*

• You've just got your husband off to work and the kids to school and have just settled down to enjoy a cup of coffee in peace when the telephone rings. It's your mother! She's not feeling well and wants to know if you will take her to see the doctor. You had planned on doing something else, and your mother's intrusion really irritates you. But what else can you do? You smile (even though she can't see you), say a few polite words, and go to get dressed. *You* are under *STRESS.*

• The boss comes to your desk with a smile on her face. "You've been doing great work," she says, "and I would like you to do a special project for me. If you do a good job, there may be other jobs like it in the future. Want to give it a try?" "Sure!" you reply with enthusiasm, and inside you feel a surge of excitement. This could be the break you've been waiting for! You get an extra cup of coffee and make arrangements to work late. *You* are under *STRESS*—even though you love your work. And if the stress is allowed to continue uninterrupted for too long, you will begin the process that leads to stress disease.

The Body's Alarm System

We live in a world that produces stress. The potential for stress is all about us—in our friends, family, work; in fact, in every part of life. And we live in bodies that are designed to respond to stress. These are two important givens of life. Each of us is equipped with a highly sophisticated defense system designed to help us cope with events in our lives that threaten and challenge us.

The stress response can be triggered by *anything* that creates a state of *arousal* or *alarm* in our bodies—anything that mobilizes our bodies' defenses against hostile, threatening, or even challenging events in our environment. (These threatening or challenging events actually don't even have to take place—it's enough just to *imagine* them!) The greater the mobilization of defense, the greater the potential for over-stress and stress damage.

When the state of alarm or emergency is triggered, our various physiological systems are bathed in adrenalin, which disrupts normal functioning and produces a heightened state of arousal. In the immediate "emergency" reaction, the heart beats faster, digestion is speeded up, and a host of hormones is released into the bloodstream to prepare us for dealing with the emergency.

We will go into these changes in a little more detail later. For now, we just need to understand that God has created us to be creatures of extreme complexity. Whenever we are threatened physically or psychologically, a complex chain of responses is set in motion to prepare us for what has been described as the "fight or flight" response. It's as simple as that. When we are under stress, our bodies are prepared either to attack what is threatening us or to run away from it.

This is the *alarm* system that is triggered by stress. Its purpose is to alert us to a threat so that we can be better equipped to deal with it. But difficulties arise when we are threatened over and over again, or when we are constantly challenged or live in a constant state of emergency. When this happens, what was designed as a protective mechanism begins to be harmful to us. We begin to experience the damaging consequences of stress.

The best way I can illustrate this is to ask you to imagine an elastic band. If it is stretched between your thumbs and then released, it returns to its normal, relaxed position as soon as the external force is removed. The body's stress response is also "stretched" whenever it is subjected to an emergency or demand. It ought to return to a normal, relaxed state when the demand is removed.

But if the elastic band is stretched and then held in an extended position for a long period of time, it begins to lose its elastic properties, develops hairline cracks, and eventually snaps. Similarly, if our bodies are repeatedly alarmed or held in a constant state of alarm, they soon begin to show damaging consequences. The so-called stress-related disorders— physical and psychological—are the consequence.

Why Does Stress Cause Illness?

While this question will also be explored more fully in the next chapter, some comments are appropriate here. Recent research suggests that one way excessive stress causes illness is by destroying the body's immunological defense mechanisms. In other words, too much stress saps the body's ability to fight off disease, so that viruses and bacteria thrive. It doesn't do it immediately, nor totally. The process takes place slowly, eventually robbing us of just enough "fighting power" to place us at jeopardy for illness. There is even some suspicion that stress may cause some forms of cancer to grow more rapidly because the body's ability to fight off the growth of cancerous cells is destroyed or diminished.

In addition to hindering the body's defense systems, stress can also lead to illness by disrupting normal functions and damaging tissue. For example, the increased secretion of acid in the stomach irritates and eats away the stomach lining and eventually may lead to inflammation or an ulcer.

There is an even more subtle way in which stress can cause illness. The high level of adrenalin found when we are under stress reduces our ability to rest, cuts down on our need to sleep, and creates poor eating habits. All of this can lead to an increase in the use of alcohol, cigarettes, and drugs. And these, in turn, can take their toll by causing further illnesses and damage in and of themselves.

Stress can set in motion a long chain of destructive side effects. Is it any wonder we are dying of it?

Not All Stress Is Bad!

But I must repeat: Stress is not damaging for everybody all the time. Sometimes we thrive on stress. We experience it as exhilaration. It fires us up and motivates us to get projects completed or to overcome obstacles.

Every athlete knows how important it is to get "psyched up" before a game. At certain times and at certain levels, stress can enhance a person's concentration, strength, creativity, and productivity. The heightened energy we get from a surge of adrenalin can even save our lives in an emergency—as it was meant to do.

But stress is only "good" if it is *short-lived*. An exciting baseball game, for instance, is time-limited! The thrill of excitement comes and goes. A challenge is met, then passes away.

This "ebb and flow" effect is crucial to keep in mind. If we never allow a calming after the storm, the storm becomes a hurricane. We must live in the valleys of low arousal in order to enjoy the mountain peaks of excitement. Good stress (also called "eustress," from the Latin *eu,* meaning good) is positive and helpful only because it is *not experienced continuously.* It excites, but then it lets the system go back to normal quickly. If a moment never comes when all the demand for stress is passed—if the body *never* returns to a state of rest and recovery—the result will be bad stress (or "distress," from the Latin *dis,* meaning bad), no matter what originally produced the arousal.

Much of the damaging stress we experience comes from threats that can't be acted on because they exist only in the mind and imagination. This kind of stress—which doesn't go away after the "game is played"—can be as dangerous as any real-life catastrophe.

Take, for example, the effect of those threats created by

worry and anxiety. There are people whose thoughts are so active and bothersome that they constantly imagine the worst. This worrying magnifies actual threats and creates imagined ones—both of which trigger the stress response. And because they *are* imagined or blown out of proportion, these threats cannot be confronted and resolved. The problem is in the mind, although for the body the threat is real. Further, we don't always recognize our "worry stressors." They hide in the dark hours of the night when we try to sleep or in the unconscious activities of our minds when we are doing our daily chores.

It is these more subtle threats that produce the greatest amount of stress damage. Things that worry us, prod us, scare or frighten us—when there is nothing we can do about them—can be the most destructive of all. Perhaps this is why Jesus (who had many good things to say about controlling stress) told us, "Let not your heart be troubled, neither let it be afraid" (John 14:27).

"Hidden" Stress

Another factor that complicates the stress picture is that we cannot always *feel* the distress we are experiencing. This is because of the amazing human trait of adaptability.

Our bodies have the remarkable ability to adjust to a wide variety of conditions—heat and cold, high and low altitudes, hard physical work or sedentary activity. For instance, if I walk into a dark room from the bright sunlight, at first I cannot see anything. But then my eyes get used to the darkness, and very soon I can see clearly. Similarly, if I now leave the dark room and go into the sunlight, I will be blinded by the bright light until my eyes adjust once again.

But there is a negative side to this wonderful ability. *Our bodies can even adapt to circumstances that in the long run are harmful to us*—such as too much stress.

For example, if stress that raises the blood pressure is imposed on the body, and if that stress is not removed after a short while, the body will adapt to this higher level of arousal just as easily as it would to living in the Sahara desert. The blood pressure will go up and stay up—and will not come down very easily again.

Simply stated, if you experience a lot of stress, your body adapts to this higher stress level; it continues to stay aroused and ready for "fight or flight." This is one reason why some people have high blood pressure even though at any given moment their life seems peaceful.

The same happens to muscle tension. It goes up when stress demands it, but doesn't necessarily come down when the stress is gone. The result can be chronic headaches, backaches, and nervous tics.

Furthermore, the "adaptation" to a higher level of stress arousal can occur in response to stressors (stress-producing factors) we don't even know exist—or at least don't recognize as being stressors. They affect us at the unconscious level, causing our bodies to react, even though we are oblivious to them.

For instance, any of the following could be causing you stress *right now* and without your knowing it:

- driving on busy freeways
- your teenager's stereo system
- living near noisy freeways or train lines
- loneliness
- complaining neighbors
- bad lighting at work or home
- too much fluorescent lighting
- opening the "childproof" type of aspirin bottles
- the neighbors' kids always coming into your garden
- bad time management
- always being late for appointments
- too many deadlines
- a spouse who won't talk
- dogs barking at night
- watching too much TV.

Any or all of these (and I'm sure you can add many to the list) can be the source of subtle, continuous, and potentially devastating stress, without our even being aware that they are causing us discomfort. Our bodies adapt to the higher arousal and give us a false sense of well-being by blotting out the discomfort. Eventually we reach the point that we are no longer capable of relaxing or returning to a nonaroused state. The first sign we may have of being under stress may be an ulcer, a headache, high blood pressure, or coronary artery disease.

Even Good Things Can Cause Bad Stress!

The greatest misunderstanding anyone can have about stress is that it is produced only by the unpleasant events of life. Many people risk unnecessary stress damage because they believe that only major catastrophes or prolonged conflict produce stress disease.

"Surely stress is only harmful when it is caused by bad things," a patient will argue after he has been referred to me by his doctor because his blood pressure is high, his headaches are frequent, and his ulcer is bleeding.

"No," I reply, "stress damage can be caused as much by the good things of life as the bad." And then I behold his puzzled amazement.

Jack is a good example. Jack is a hard-working, highly driven attorney. At thirty-four years of age, he is considered tops in his field. He loves his work, savoring the thrill of each new challenge. He is happiest when a crisis or emergency requires him to work intensely on a special project.

If you were to ask Jack whether he was experiencing stress, he would quickly deny it. He's happy. He's in good shape; he plays handball three times a week. He enjoys his young family and spends time with them. He would insist there is nothing in his life to cause him stress.

Then one morning Jack is awakened in the early hours

by an uncomfortable feeling in his chest. His heart seems to be skipping beats and he has difficulty getting enough air, even though he is breathing rapidly. An intense panic sets in; he wonders, "Am I having a heart attack?" He lies there still and quiet, not wanting to alarm his wife. After awhile the bad feeling passes and he finally falls asleep.

The next day Jack decides to see his doctor for a checkup. No, he wasn't having a heart attack. Yes, he is in good health, except that his blood pressure is up.

"What is wrong, then?" he asks the doctor.

"You are under too much stress," the doctor says to a very puzzled Jack.

Jack is experiencing a common variety of panic disorder brought on by the overexcitement of his body's stress response system. *And this overexcitement can be caused just as easily by doing something pleasurable as by experiencing something painful or unpleasant.* The body really can't tell the difference.

Dr. Hans Selye, the father of stress research (and the originator of the terms *eustress* and *distress*), made this clear when he defined stress as "the *nonspecific* response of the body to *any* demand." He emphasizes that the body can respond in the same manner to *many* types of pressure—both good and bad. The excitement of getting married or watching the home team play a winning game can produce as much stress as struggling to meet a publisher's deadline or facing an angry boss. Although the one causes good stress (eustress) and the other bad stress (distress), both make the same demands on certain parts of the body and move you away from your normal resting equilibrium. Too much of *either* type over an extended period of time can work havoc in your body.

Dr. Selye made this discovery many years ago while performing an experiment with laboratory rats. The story of his discovery is worth repeating because it vividly shows how *all* stress—regardless of origin—affects the body.

In his early experiments with hormone chemistry, Dr. Selye

was trying to isolate the effects of individual hormones on laboratory rats. Hormones are the body's chemical messengers, carried through the blood to all the organs, and Dr. Selye wanted to find out precisely how each chemical affected the animal's body. So he injected various prepared substances into a number of rats.

What Dr. Selye discovered was very confusing at first. He found that no matter what the hormone was, the internal damage it caused in the rats was *always the same*. Extensive purifying of the chemicals made no difference. Neither did using combinations of hormones.

Three rather dramatic effects occurred within the bodies of all the animals he had injected with hormones: (1) the adrenal glands were enlarged to a marked degree—swollen from overactivity; (2) the thymus gland, responsible for helping the rat fight off disease, had atrophied; and (3) the animal had developed ulcers.

Dr. Selye puzzled over these strange results for quite awhile. Then he had one of those "aha" experiences that every researcher dreams about. He realized the experiment was showing that *anything* which challenges the body's equilibrium will put it into an emergency mode of responding, and the result over a period of time will be stress damage.

We will see a little later how the specific results of this experiment explain the ways stress effects us physically. For now, it will serve to illustrate the crucial point that stress doesn't have to come from unpleasant or negative sources to be bad for us. Excitement and challenge can kill us just as easily as sadness and fear.

I would even venture to say that the positive, pleasant stresses in life are *more* likely to lead to stress disease. This is one thing that makes stress disease so mysterious and dangerous. Of course, a major trauma like a divorce will contribute its share of damage, just as will being out of work or having a son go off the rails and get in trouble with the law. But these "big problems" of life are usually time-limited. They are confined to a span of weeks or perhaps months, and sooner or later they pass off the scene. We *want* to get them out of our lives as soon as possible.

The other—the more challenging or pleasant demands—can stay with us a long time. Like water dripping on a stone, they may eventually wear us down.

In truth, this is only a part of the stress story, but it is a very important part because it is so easy to overlook. While severe physical or emotional distress can cause significant stress damage, there is a hidden enemy lurking beneath the turbulent waters of excitement and challenge. By far the greater amount of stress damage today is brought about not by major life traumas, but by agreeable experiences, exciting challenges, or stimulating competition. Until we grasp this central truth, we will never be masters of our stress.

What Causes Us Stress?

In summary, let me review the many causes of stress in our lives. Stress can result from anything that:

- annoys you
- threatens you
- prods you
- excites you
- scares you
- worries you
- hurries you
- angers you
- frustrates you
- challenges you
- criticizes you
- reduces your self-esteem.

Anything—pleasant or unpleasant—that arouses your adrenalin system and mobilizes your body for "fight or flight," then doesn't let up and allow time for recovery can predispose you to stress disease. Your body simply adapts to living in a constant state of emergency—and you feel no discomfort until damaging results occur.

So this is the problem of stress—and I have only told part of the story! The real problem is that most people don't realize they've got a problem! Or if they do acknowledge it, they are not sure what to do about it. I hope that as you proceed with me you will soon have a better understanding of how you can reduce the damage done by stress in your life.

2

How Stress
Does Its Damage

If you clench your fist and place it at the center of your breastbone, then imagine it is colored pinkish gray and acting like it owned your body, you have just pictured your heart.

The heart is a remarkable organ. It stands at the very core of life, and its beat is central to survival. Believe it or not, every day the heart pumps about two thousand gallons of blood (the equivalent of a hundred large automobile gasoline tanks) through sixty thousand miles of elastic tubing.

Is it any wonder that the Bible has so much to say about the heart? It is pictured not only as the seat of life (Prov. 4:23), but also as the determiner of character (Matt. 15:18) and of faith (Rom. 10:10). It has both biological and spiritual meanings in Scripture because it is so central to life itself.

The "Heart" of the Stress Problem

There is one other important characteristic of the heart that we should be aware of when it comes to stress. *The heart is the central target of destruction for much of the harmful stress we experience.*

Dr. Jay Cohn, head of the cardiovascular division of the University of Minnesota Medical School, says, "The heart is actually an incredibly intelligent organ. When you walk up a flight of stairs, when you get nervous or excited, or when someone scares you, your heart immediately responds with changes in rate, force, and contraction." [1] Even when we

---

1. Quoted in *Science Digest*, April 1985, p. 31.

transplant a heart, it still has this incredible ability to adjust its performance to a change of home. It can go on functioning in another person's chest as if it had always lived there!

How does it do this? It has no direct connections to the nervous system to receive signals from the brain, but it *is* designed to respond to signals from the complex *chemical messengers* circulating in the blood—including the adrenalin hormones. Unfortunately, this sensitivity to chemical messengers carries with it risks as well as advantages. Over a period of time, when out of balance, these messengers can literally destroy the heart.

Heart disease is the twentieth century's major health problem—an estimated 62.7 million Americans suffer from it. According to the American Heart Association, nearly a million Americans die each year from heart attacks, strokes, and other illnesses related to the cardiovascular system. This is more than all the other causes of death—including cancer, car accidents, and infections—*put together.* Many others survive but are left disabled or paralyzed.

Only seventy or eighty years ago, heart disease was less of a risk, being only the fourth leading cause of death. It is because we have brought many other diseases under control that we now live longer and experience a greater risk of heart disease. In a sense, a greater incidence of heart disease is an indication of blessings brought about by the progress of modern medicine. But there is no reason at all why we cannot also bring heart disease under control if we deal with the essential cause of it.

Causes of Heart Disease

Because heart disease is such an important consequence of stress in general, we need to pay particular attention to it. Certain risk factors for heart disease are now well known. These include:

- a family history of heart disease and male gender
- cigarette smoking (Stopping smoking, however, can eventually reverse the risk.)

- high blood pressure (called the "silent killer")
- high blood cholesterol level, especially high levels of the low-density lipoproteins (LDLs), causing the narrowing and hardening of the arteries (for more on cholesterol, see chapter 7).

But is this the total picture? Or is it possible that *behind* all these factors is *one* single enemy? I believe so. As we will see, there is abundant evidence to support the idea that excessive circulating *adrenalin* lies behind all of these other risk factors. This is one reason cardiovascular problems often run in families, because we can inherit (or learn from an early age) our predisposition to higher adrenalin arousal.

The truth is that the most common cause of heart disease by far is "atherosclerosis" (from the Greek words for "gruel" and "hardening"), which involves the progressive hardening of the arteries with a build-up of plaque. This disease is thought to begin *early in life* and significantly affects about half the population at the time of death.

What is the cause of atherosclerosis? There is still much we don't know, but there is enough evidence to suggest that one of the culprits is the excessive recruitment of adrenalin— the body's emergency hormone.

Most of us must live in highly competitive and demanding life situations. This begins at an early age and keeps us constantly on the move, striving for greater things. In fact, many of us live our whole lives in what is essentially a state of emergency and hurry. And we become dependent on overproduction of adrenalin for our accomplishments. But we pay for this later with accelerated wear and tear on our cardiovascular systems.

This is why the kind of person who is always in a hurry, who has low tolerance for frustration, and who is highly driven is at such great risk for heart disease. (We will discuss this personality type—known as "Type A," in the next chapter.) This kind of person is known to produce significantly higher levels of circulating adrenalin and related stress hormones. You can't live in a constant state of emergency and not pay for it physically.

Other Kinds of Stress Damage

Of course, stress disease is not confined to the heart. It attacks many parts of the body. While the other symptoms of stress are not always as life threatening as heart disease, they certainly have a negative effect on the quality of our lives. Vast numbers of people suffer from stress symptoms such as headaches, ulcers, digestive problems, or muscle spasms and are living *very* painful lives. They are dependent on medication simply to function. And some will even tell you, quite frankly, that living as they do is not much better than being dead!

I strongly feel that depending solely on medication to alleviate stress symptoms is not adequate treatment. It is like closing the barn door after the horse has bolted. It is treating the symptom but not the disease. But how can we become less dependent on drugs for protection against stress disease? How can we begin to reduce or eliminate the debilitating effects of stress? I believe a very important way to do this is to become more aware of how the body recruits adrenalin in response to stress.

Understanding the Stress Response

Take a moment to study figure 1 on p. 36. Notice that stress can originate in either external or internal events.

While we do experience much of our stress from outside forces we cannot control, a lot of this outside stress comes from how we *perceive* the world around us. (It is what we *think* about what is happening to us—our *interpretation* of the outside world, not just the world itself—that causes us the most stress.) External stressors include threats, adversity, and conflict as well as excitement or challenge.

Other stress originates on the *inside.* Illness, physical handicaps, and discomfort can produce stress as readily as external threats or catastrophe.

I recently had to undergo surgery. For the three or four

FIGURE 1
The Stress Response

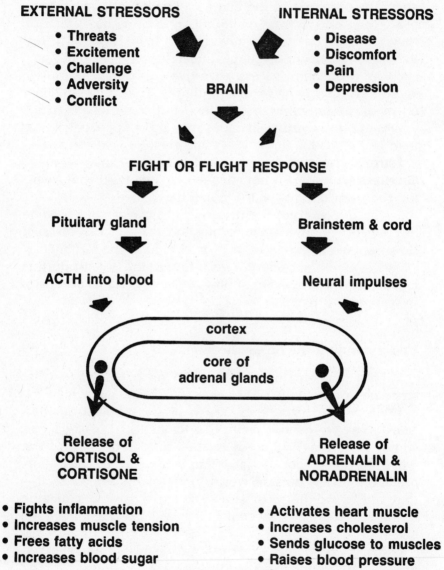

EXTERNAL STRESSORS
- Threats
- Excitement
- Challenge
- Adversity
- Conflict

INTERNAL STRESSORS
- Disease
- Discomfort
- Pain
- Depression

BRAIN

FIGHT OR FLIGHT RESPONSE

Pituitary gland

Brainstem & cord

ACTH into blood

Neural impulses

cortex
core of
adrenal glands

Release of
CORTISOL &
CORTISONE

Release of
ADRENALIN &
NORADRENALIN

- Fights inflammation
- Increases muscle tension
- Frees fatty acids
- Increases blood sugar

- Activates heart muscle
- Increases cholesterol
- Sends glucose to muscles
- Raises blood pressure
- Increases heart rate

weeks following, I monitored my body very closely and discovered that, while the surgery wound was healing quite well, I was experiencing many symptoms of stress during the recovery period. Even the process of healing was stressful to me.

The body doesn't distinguish between whether a stressor is from within or from without—it responds in the same way. What happens is that the brain sends messages along two separate pathways. The first is to the pituitary gland, which releases a substance called "adrenocorticotrophic hormone," or ACTH for short. ACTH in turn stimulates the adrenal glands. (The term *adrenal* literally means "toward kidney," from the Latin *ad renal*. The glands were so named because one is located on top of each kidney.)

The second pathway is through the brain stem and spinal cord, which send nerve impulses to many parts of the body, including the adrenal glands.

The combined effect of these chemical and neural signals is to stimulate the two major parts of the adrenal gland—the "core" and the "cortex."

The cortex releases many hormones, but the two important ones are cortisol and cortisone, both of which, at normal levels of arousal, help fight pain and inflammation. It is the core that releases adrenalin and noradrenalin into the bloodstream; these hormones stimulate the heart, raise the blood pressure, and prepare us for the unique emergency reaction in the body to which I have already alluded—the "fight or flight" response. We are physically prepared either to attack the source of our stress or to run away from it.

The effect of this "fight or flight" response on the rest of the body is extremely important to understand. If we follow this response through its intricate and intertwined pathway, we can readily see how the various symptoms of prolonged stress are created.

The increase demand for blood in the brain (to mobilize us for action) means that the *heart* has to do extra work. The *muscles* (to provide a quick getaway or more force in fighting) and the *stomach* (to digest food and provide needed energy) also demand extra blood, which then has to be withdrawn from other parts of the body where it is not needed as much. For example, the reduced circulation of blood in the hands causes the "cold hands" phenomenon so often experienced by those under stress. Later in this book, we will use the monitoring of the "cold hands" reaction as a way of recognizing adrenalin arousal.

The increased activity in the stomach, especially when stress is chronic, often gives rise to ulcers (because of increased acid secretion) and a host of other gastrointestinal complaints. The increased tension in the muscles can cause pain after awhile and is the underlying factor in many headaches and backaches.

In section 2 we will discuss in more detail the wide variety of symptoms that can be brought on by prolonged stress. But what is important for us to understand here is how the emergency response system of the body can create a state of increased activity throughout the body—all because the "stress hormones," especially adrenalin, are circulating in the bloodstream and carrying their messages of arousal.

The Effects of Elevated Adrenalin

The chronic increased flow of adrenalin produces a number of other, more serious, consequences. These include:

- an increase in the production of blood cholesterol
- a narrowing of the capillaries and other blood vessels that can shut down the blood supply to the heart muscle
- a decrease in the body's ability to remove cholesterol
- an increase in the blood's tendency to clot
- an increase in the depositing of plaque on the walls of the arteries.

In short bursts, elevated adrenalin is *not* damaging or dangerous, but when sustained at high levels over a period of time it can be very harmful. Adrenalin arousal can be compared to revving up an engine and then leaving it to idle. Idling an engine on high for a short period of time clears out gum deposits and dirty carbon. But when the engine is left idling for a long time, carbon deposits collect in the valves. The engine wears out faster.

This is more or less what happens in the heart when there is a prolonged and chronic elevation of adrenalin. The adrenalin keeps the system moving at a high speed, and deterioration occurs at a faster rate. We actually age faster.

However, since an elevated adrenalin level can also give a person a heightened sense of well-being, increased energy, reduced need for sleep, and feelings of excitement or even euphoria, we are often completely unaware this destruction is taking place. It is easy to see why many become addicted to this state of arousal. The feelings of security it provides can give one a dangerously false sense of well-being.

Once more: The most serious effect of elevated adrenalin, when persistent and unrelenting, is its damage to the heart and arteries. Drs. Meyer Friedman and Ray Rosenman, the cardiologists who identified the personality type most prone to heart disease, clearly indicate from their research the connection between prolonged adrenalin arousal and heart disease. They state:

> The chronic excess discharge and circulation of the catecholamines (adrenalin and noradrenalin). . . . may be the chief factor in the total process of arterial decay and thrombosis. We have seen coronary heart disease erupt in many subjects whose blood insulin levels and metabolism of cholesterol, fat, and sugar were quite normal. But rarely have we ever witnessed the onset of this disease in a person whose rate of manufacture and secretion of catecholamines (adrenalin and noradrenalin) we did not know or suspect to have been increased.[2]

2. Meyer Friedman and Ray Rosenman, *Type-A Behavior and Your Heart* (New York: Knopf, 1974) p. 178.

Learning to Live on Less Adrenalin

What does all this mean? Simply this. To avoid cardiovascular disease and other stress-related disorders, it is not enough to eat the right food and keep cholesterol levels low. It is not enough to exercise regularly and even to take regular vacations. To protect ourselves against dying of or suffering ill effects from stress, we must learn how to switch off our production of adrenalin when it is no longer needed. We've got to become less dependent on the energy hormone for everyday living.

Since anger, frustration, irritation, challenge, and excitement are all adrenalin triggers, these psychological triggers must be brought under control. Effective stress management requires that we be healthy in mind and spirit, not just in our bodies. This is what I mean by "adrenalin management." It means controlling the problem at its source.

If you love excitement and enjoy the thrill of challenge, you will have to work a little harder at controlling your adrenalin—because you have a greater tendency to produce too much of it. You may have to work at learning to enjoy life without constant novel stimulation. You will have to train yourself to come down frequently from the "mountaintop" and enjoy the peace of the valley, where recuperation and healing can take place. In later chapters of this book I will be showing some specific, practical ways you can do this.

The accelerated pace of modern living tends to rob us of natural recovery time, so that must be planned into our lives by deliberate design. Even Jesus was aware of this need for recovery. In Mark 6:31, he told his disciples, "Come ye yourselves apart into a desert place, and rest a while: for there were many coming and going, and they had no leisure so much as to eat."

If Jesus thought it necessary for him and his disciples to rest from time to time, who are we to think we can get by without it?

3

Stress as "Hurry Sickness"

I have a friend about my age who is also a psychologist. He lives in another part of the country, so I don't get to see him often. What makes this friend very special is that he is almost a mirror image of me! I don't mean that we look alike, since he's much more handsome and athletic than I am. No, I mean that we tend to *behave* very much alike, and because of this we understand each other very well. He gets angry at the same things I do. He becomes impatient in the same kinds of situations that make me impatient. And he becomes restless when he has nothing to do—just like me!

What we have in common is known as a "Type-A" personality.

My friend suffered from a severe heart attack six years ago, and he has never been the same since. He is much better! He has learned to be more sensitive to his personal needs, as well as becoming more patient, more loving, and more spiritual. And because I can relate to my friend so well, his attack has helped *me* to be a lot more level-headed also.

The Type-A Personality

The idea that there is a particular type of personality that is more prone to experience distress is now widely accepted, although of course it must be recognized that not everybody can be put into a simple two-box category. In fact, most people are really a mixture of many characteristics. But for our purpose it can be helpful to think of ourselves as fitting into one category or the other. No doubt you have heard many references to these personality categories—"Type A" and "Type B" (with those people who seem to have an even mixture of the two being labeled "Type X"). Sometimes such a category is called "Type-A (or B) personality"; at other times it is "Type-A (or B) behavior pattern" or simply "TABP" (or "TBBP").

I should also say at this point that some researchers do take issue with this simple classification system. For example, H. J. Eysenk, a British psychologist, believes that Type-A qualities such as tenseness, ambition, and activity are found in varying degrees in all of us. But again, the important thing at this point is not putting people in categories but understanding how stress affects us and having some way of telling whether we lean strongly or weakly in the direction of trouble. And in my experience the tool of personality categorization has been very helpful.

What are the traits displayed by those who are predominately Type A? Type-A behavior is an "action-emotion complex" that can be seen in those persons who are always struggling to achieve more and more in less and less time. In essence, they are always in a hurry.

Of course, there are other characteristics that describe the Type-A person as well. Some of these are:
- They have a high degree of competitiveness.
- They are easily irritated by delays.
- They have a low tolerance for frustration.
- They are hard-driving and ambitious.
- They are highly aggressive.
- They are easily angered and often have free-floating hostility.
- They cannot relax without feeling guilty.
- They are confident on the surface but insecure within.
- They speak aggressively, accentuating key words.
- They have a tendency to finish other people's sentences.

What percentage of the population is Type A? This is a hard question to answer. Estimates range from 50 percent to 70 percent, depending on how personality types are measured and whether the population being studied is urban or rural. Type Bs seem to be less prominent in our large cities.

I experience my Type-A pattern quite readily whenever I go to the supermarket. I usually go for a long bicycle ride in the evening. When I do, my wife often asks me to stop at the supermarket and buy a few things. After I've loaded the shopping basket with the milk, fruit, bread, and a few other needs, I go to the "express lane" check-out. The sign says "cash only—no more than twelve items." I stand there looking at the people ahead of me and start to become impatient. I count the items in their baskets. (Woe betide anyone who exceeds twelve items!) I become restless and ask myself, "Why is this express line the slowest of all?" I look at the regular check-out lines. They always seem to be going faster. Finally my turn comes, and with a great sense of relief I leave the supermarket resolving never to be frustrated again—until I go there the next evening!

Type-B people, on the other hand, are relatively free of most of the habits I have described above. They do not feel bound by time, have less sense of urgency, and find time to play and relax. They are less concerned about what peers and superiors may think about their actions, and they have resigned themselves to the restrictions that their humanness places upon them.

Type Bs may appear to be the "tortoises" of our world alongside the Type-A "rabbits," but this isn't altogether a fair analogy. Many Type Bs are high achievers and are in positions of responsibility. They are energetic and fast when the task demands it, but they can "switch off" and take it easy when the crisis is over!

Of course, no person is a pure Type A or Type B. Most of us are a blend of the two. But this categorization helps to point up our predominating characteristics. Figure 2 presents a brief test for Type-A personality so that you can determine what your predominant personality type is. (The key for interpreting your "score" is found in Appendix 1 at the end of this book.)

The Penalty for Type-A Tendencies

There are some good things about being a Type-A person. People with this personality type accomplish a lot. They get things done. And often their sense of hurry comes from caring deeply about and feeling responsible for the world around them.

But there is a physical penalty to be paid for being a predominantly Type-A person. Type-A people recruit very much more adrenalin than Type B. And research has shown that Type-A men have *three times* the incidence of heart disease as Type-B men. This is rapidly becoming true of women, also, as they move into a more competitive lifestyle.

What is important to remember is that the stress hormones, including adrenalin, are always found in *excessive* amounts in these individuals. Type-A behavior patterns and higher levels of adrenalin are lifelong partners.

Since the Type-A and Type-B descriptions of personality have been well discussed in other books on stress, it is not my intention to focus on these personality traits in any depth here. In this chapter, I want to focus on the one characteristic of the Type-A behavior pattern that I believe to be the most neglected and therefore the most dangerous of all—the sense of *time urgency* that gives rise to what I call "hurry sickness." And I want to look at the ways this time urgency has permeated the lives of all of us, creating what could almost be called a Type-A culture! So it is important to understand what "Type-A-ness" is about—even if you are more of a Type B. Doing so may help you withstand the pressures you feel all around you to become more of a Type A.

FIGURE 2
Type-A Behavior Pattern Test

Read each question carefully and give yourself a rating according to the following descriptions:

Rating	Description
0	This statement does not apply to me.
1	It sometimes (less than once a month) applies to me.
2	It often (more than once a month) applies to me.

STATEMENT	RATING
1. I feel as if there isn't enough time in each day to do all the things I need to do.	2
2. I tend to speak faster than other people, even finishing their sentences for them.	1
3. My spouse or friends say, or I believe, that I eat too quickly.	1
4. I tend to get very upset whenever I lose a game.	0
5. I am very competitive in work, sports, or games.	1
6. I tend to be bossy and dominate others.	1
7. I prefer to lead rather than follow.	2
8. I feel pressed for time even when I am not doing something important.	2
9. I become impatient when I have to wait.	1
10. I tend to make decisions quickly, even impulsively.	1
11. I regularly take on more than I can accomplish.	2
12. I become irritable (even angry) more often than most other people.	2
TOTAL	16

Handwritten annotations in left margin: 1, 2, 2, 2, 2, 1, 1, 2, 2, 0, 2, 2, 19

Handwritten annotations in right margin: 2, 2, 2, 0, 0, 2, 7, 2, 1, 0, 1, 0, 13

Hurry Sickness—A Twentieth-Century Disease

A large part of the damage we experience in our lives is basically "hurry sickness." It comes from our urge to live and do everything in a hurry. As a consequence, we are living at a pace too fast for our bodies. This hurried lifestyle creates an internal state of emergency that elevates our adrenalin.

At least 50 percent—probably a bit more—of the characteristics of the Type-A behavior pattern can be accounted for by the idea of "hurriedness." Type-A persons constantly struggle against time. They hate to "waste time" for eating, having a haircut, or sitting in the park. They are always active, restless, moving, doing things. And Type-A people pay for their sense of time urgency in increased circulation of adrenalin and consequent stress damage.

But there's another aspect to hurry sickness that transcends basic tendencies and personality types. For hurry has become a distinguishing characteristic of the age we live in. Type As and Type Bs alike are constantly bombarded by demands to do more and more—faster and faster. Expanded opportunities and enhanced communication also mean constant stimulation and demand. And while Type As probably react more strongly to this dominant culture, none of us is immune to it.

This raises an interesting question. Have humans always suffered from hurry sickness? I teach many stress management seminars to ministers and missionaries. One of the questions most frequently asked is, "Why were great preachers like John Wesley and Charles Spurgeon not bothered by stress disease? They worked long hours, gave of themselves unselfishly, and sacrificed many luxuries. Yet they seemed to be free of what bothers us." (Actually, Spurgeon suffered from deep depressions, but the question is still a valid one.)

My answer is usually quite simple: These men lived in a different age. Hurry sickness is largely a phenomenon of the twentieth century. It began with the industrial revolution and has continued to increase right up to the present.

The pace of life has accelerated dramatically in the past forty or fifty years. Most of us barely find time to brush our teeth, let alone spend time in relaxation, meditation, or prayer. Our culture is oriented toward speed and efficiency; it is hard to succeed unless you move as fast as everyone else. And I am as guilty of being caught up in this rat race as anyone!

Consider for a moment what life was like in previous times. A few thousand years ago, the fastest most people could travel was on foot, or perhaps on the back of a donkey or camel— about four or five miles an hour. A chariot could take you between cities at about twenty miles an hour, but only a few could enjoy this luxury. Today, however, we can all travel at quite fantastic speeds in automobiles and airplanes. No doubt we'll be able to speed normal transportation up further with bullet trains and underground zip tubes.

Gone is the leisurely, slow-paced way of life that once existed. We no longer have much time for reflection or—more important—time to allow our bodies to relax so that restoration and healing can take place. In past times, without electricity, evenings were calm and unstimulated, allowing the adrenalin system to "switch off." But today there is hardly any moment when we are not being bombarded with stimuli—from the moment we wake up until, exhausted, we switch off late-night television. The toll our fast-paced lives takes on our adrenal systems is quite frightening—and mostly unacknowledged.

In Christ's time, oil was expensive. So when the sun went down, the day stopped for everyone. Nighttime was for resting, and this allowed adequate recovery time for people's bodies. This, coupled with plenty of physical outlets, ensured that stress was not the threat to health and happiness that it is today. (True, people died young, but because of disease and poor sanitary conditions, not because of stress!)

I was brought up in Africa, and know something of life in a more primitive culture. African culture has always fascinated me because, in many respects, it has taught me a number of important lessons about my modern lifestyle. It has helped me, for instance, to get a better understanding of how people lived in New Testament times. It has also helped me to put my Western culture in its proper perspective and live a more balanced life.

For Westerners, the indifference to time displayed by most Africans is maddening. Church services seldom start on time. They go on for hours and certainly never end when they are supposed to. Africans are just not hooked on time!

My digital wristwatch, the most modern available to me, can tell me the time up to a hundredth of a second. Most Africans can tell time by the sun to the nearest hour. I suffer from being under a lot of stress! They seldom do. Sometimes I almost wish I could trade my Seiko for a sundial.

About a year ago I was scheduled to speak at a conference in Chicago. I went to my office on a Friday morning, saw three patients, drove to Los Angeles International Airport, flew to Chicago, and got there in time to address an evening meeting. I spoke three times on Saturday and twice on Sunday, then flew back to Los Angeles in time to get to bed. The next morning I went to work as usual.

Such hectic, "rush about" activity takes a heavy stress toll on one's body. And needless to say, four days later I came down with a severe influenza attack—attributable, I believe, to a case of overextension and overstress. My immune system had simply given out.

You see, God designed my body for camel travel and I keep putting it in subsonic jets! Camel travel allows plenty of time for rest. Subsonic flying keeps me tense and stressed.

Now, I am *not* saying that we should give up flying in jets! I thank God for them every day that I travel. But I am saying we need to recognize that the human frame has its limits, and that we should build in adequate rest and recovery time so as to allow healing and restoration to take place.

This is the problem: People in a hurry never have time for recovery. Their minds have little time to meditate and pray so that problems can be put in perspective. In short, people in our age are showing signs of physiological disinte-gration because we are living at a pace that is too fast for our bodies. *This is the essence of the stress problem.*

Changes in Our Lives Makes Us Stress-Prone

Not only do most of us live life in the fast lane where we have little time for real rest, but social and moral values are changing so rapidly that trying to remain in harmony with God's universal and eternal standards is becoming more and more stressful. My daughters often remind me how much pressure they get from peers to "go with the crowd" or to throw away their Christian values. Being a Christian can be very tough going in today's world.

And our lives are changing in other ways that keep our stress levels high. For one thing, we are becoming more and more of a mobile society. It is estimated, for example, that the average adult makes six job-related moves during a life-time. And each move is a major upheaval requiring buying or renting a home, changing schools for the children, adjust-ing to new friends, finding new physicians, locating a church home.

These changes and others like them can be so stressful that some researchers point to "life change"—both positive and negative—as a significant measure of how much stress a person is undergoing.

After studying many patients who had undergone life change ranging from minor to significant, Drs. Tom Holmes and Richard Rahe developed a scale measuring the stress value of these events and assigned corresponding point values to each of them. Holmes and Rahe then followed their sub-jects' progress for two years and found that anyone undergo-ing significant life change became prone to illness. The greater the number and severity of changes (as indicated by a high "score" on the scale), the greater the risk for illness. And it didn't matter whether it was good life change or bad. It was the *change* that caused the stress.

Change demands adjustment, and adjustment causes adrenalin arousal. Our complex lives, with the many demands for change that confront us so frequently, can significantly increase our susceptibility to stress damage.

Turning Bad Stress into Good Stress

It would be unfair of me to suggest that all challenge, change, excitement, and fervor for work or play should be avoided because it is stressful. This is not my intention, nor would it be a completely accurate picture.

Life is to be *lived*—and lived to the *fullest.* Being highly motivated to accomplish some task and able to work with enthusiasm is a great blessing. To experience the flood of energy that propels one into action to meet a need, make a deadline, or accomplish a demanding task is what makes life worthwhile. Without such challenges we might as well be dead. Progress in medicine would slow to a snail's pace, the gospel would never reach the unreached, and justice for the oppressed would never get a vote.

Nothing worthwhile can be accomplished without arousal of the stress response system. It is a biological law that we must fight and work for a worthwhile goal. Challenge and fulfillment are important to health and well-being. But— and this point is critical—challenges and stress *must* be accompanied by and work in harmony with relaxation and rest.

This raises a very important question. Is there really such a thing as *good stress?* In chapter 1 we tried to differentiate between harmful "distress" and helpful, healthy "eustress." But here we encounter a problem, because we also saw that under *any* stress the body undergoes virtually the same reaction. What then makes the difference between good and bad stress?

There are two important answers:

- Eustress—healthy stress—results when we adapt to our stressors and successfully cope with them.

• Eustress—healthy stress—results when we quickly bring our systems back to a state of rest and low arousal.

To tell the truth, I am almost afraid to admit there is such a thing as good stress, for fear that doing so might perpetuate excuses to continue living over-hurried lives. Too many of us hide behind the belief that "some pressure is good for us" and rationalize our hectic and hurried lives with: "But I am enjoying what I do—so it must be healthy," or "But I don't feel anxious, so I can't be under all that much stress."

This is a delusion. I have known quite a few people who have died from heart attacks. And most of these people enjoyed *up to the last minute* the process that led to the destruction of their cardiovascular systems. Remember, adrenal arousal is seldom unpleasant; it invigorates and excites while it wears our systems down.

This is why it is necessary to emphasize over and over the importance of *rest* in avoiding stress damage. Bad stress can become good *only* if we bring ourselves back to a state of calmness as soon as possible. Good stress must have this pattern about it on an hourly, daily, and weekly basis: High adrenalin arousal must be allowed when demanded, but then be brought back to a state of low arousal afterward.

The pattern should look like a series of hills and valleys. Every mountain of high arousal should be followed by a valley of recuperation. Each day should end with a return to low arousal. Each challenge of the day should end with a calming of the body. And each week of work should end with rest. If you can do this, you will be healthy in body, mind, and spirit—and all your stress will be "good." You will be obedient to God's laws for your total person and this will bring you health.

Whatever we may believe theologically about the Sabbath that was instituted under the Old Covenant, the benefits to be derived from a strict observance of it are tremendous in terms of protecting us from stress and turning bad stress into good stress. Most modern-day Christians work harder on their day of worship than they do on regular work days. They have many activities planned, and many church services are designed toward stimulation and excitement rather than prayer and meditation. Adrenalin flows as strongly during these devotional times as it does during the rest of the week. (And this is not even to mention preachers and ministers, whose primary week's work is done on Sunday!)

Once again, we all need some stress to keep us functioning at our maximum effectiveness and to do worthwhile things in our world. But too much stress is harmful to us. The key word is *balance*, with lots of relaxation thrown in for good measure.

The Antidote for Hurry Sickness

Hurry sickness is a killer of innocent people—people who don't know that the disease does its damage insidiously and right before their eyes. In their haste they are oblivious to it and even encourage it through ignorance.

Our culture, especially those of us who fit the Type-A personality profile, tends to have a warped perspective about time. On one hand, we think of it as "the enemy," and we're always trying to "beat the clock." But on the other hand we almost seem to worship time. We place big clocks on tall steeples where we can all stare at them, then attach large bells that can clang out the hours to remind us how little we are accomplishing.

There was an era when the reminder of the passage of time was helpful in *slowing* us down. "There's lots of time," I can remember my grandfather saying as the big clock in the hall chimed ten in the morning. "Let's take a break and go fishing down at the river." These days my digital wristwatch beeps to remind me that the hour is up; I say to a patient, "Time is gone; I need to hurry on to my next client." And my stomach doesn't feel quite the same as it did when my grandfather's clock did the chiming.

From time to time we have all experienced that feeling

of renewal that comes from a period of rest. Perhaps a vacation—or even a forced illness—slowed us down and we found a new sense of inner peace. Freed from deadlines, demands, and conflicts, we "let down" and discovered a new self.

A few years ago I enjoyed one of those privileges given to those in academics—a sabbatical year. Free of regular duties, I could devote myself to reading, study, writing, and in-depth devotions. My wife attests to the fact that after the third month I was a different person. Free of any race with time, I mellowed. I walked and talked more slowly, and I seemed more at peace. I know I felt new sensations and became more alert and attentive to the world around me. I even got to know our neighbors.

When I came to the end of my sabbatical, one big question hung in my mind. Was I going to go back to being my old self? Would "hurry sickness" invade my soul? Would I go back to gulping down my food, talking rapidly, and ignoring the birds in my garden? I resolved I wouldn't, and my wife says that in the three years since my sabbatical I *have* been different. My attitude toward delays has changed; my reaction to frustrating people has mellowed; and I am able to control my sense of urgency rather than letting it control me. I feel more efficient, my thinking is clearer, and I am content with my accomplishments. Sometimes I speed up to meet a deadline, but mostly I try to savor every morsel of time.

Once more, let me reiterate my main point: I am not advocating that we disengage from life and ignore its challenges. I am also not suggesting that we give up the race for success and retreat to a state of nonachievement. What I *am* emphasizing is that right in the middle of our hectic, hurried lives we learn how to slow down when necessary and build in relaxation and rest time. I'll have more to say about this later.

One great lesson I am learning is that while I can travel with God in the city and on busy freeways as much as in the country or desert, it is easier to keep close to him when I am not hurrying. Meeting the demands of modern-day life head-on without ever slowing down is disastrous. Hitting each day at supersonic speed without ever taking time to slow down will burn out our body engines.

Why not learn to move at God's pace? He is never too fast, nor is he ever too slow. And he can give us the balance we need to build resistance to stress disease.

4

Stress and the Spirit

For the Christian, both the prevention and cure of stress disease needs to be informed by a biblical perspective. After all, it is our attitude and manner of living that determine to the greatest extent whether the stress in our lives becomes damaging distress. If we live godly and God-directed lives, I believe we will be healthier and more balanced in our living.

Stress Versus the Spirit

What does being a Christian have to say about living under stress? And what effect does overstress have on our spiritual lives? I think these are important questions because my experience has shown that there is a very close relationship between a person's spiritual life and the amount of harmful stress he or she experiences.

Let's take Andy as an example. Andy is a typical Type-A personality. He has been a dentist for fifteen years in a small neighborhood practice where his father was a dentist before him. He works hard, but time is his enemy. He is always racing against the clock. He schedules a patient every fifteen or twenty minutes with no time for a break in between. Often he works right through his lunch hour.

Andy is also an active church member. He has been a Christian since his late teens, when he responded to a call for commitment at a youth rally. He gives himself to church duties on a Sunday just as intensely as he does to his work.

He has four or five responsibilities at church, including being leader of his adult class and a member of the board of deacons.

"There is only one thing I lack," Andy tells me as we try to help his recovery after heart surgery. "I don't feel very spiritual. Deep down I feel empty."

Is Andy alone in this? I believe not. There is something about hurry sickness that works against our spiritual development. My close association with many pastors confirms this, and what I have learned in my own struggles certainly underlines it. The Spirit of God has little affinity with our hurried, hassled, hasty, and heartless way of living.

The words of Proverbs 19:2 are very wise: "He that hasteth with his feet sinneth." We can easily miss God's path for us when we move too quickly!

The Spiritual Consequences of Stress

In earlier chapters we have seen that stress produces *physical* consequences, since most of the outwardly recognizable symptoms of distress occur in our bodies. We know that continuous stimulation of our endocrine system eventually results in increased susceptibility to disease and accelerated wear and tear on our bodies.

We also know that too much stress produces *psychological* consequences. When we are overstressed, we become irritable, depressed, frustrated, and very anxious. Anxiety makes us less able to cope with stress, and this in turn creates more stress and more anxiety.

But I believe stress has *spiritual* consequences also. And I want to suggest three ways in which overstress can cause us to suffer spiritually:

(1) *Overstress diminishes spiritual energy.* We all have some amount of spiritual "appetite," although some of us have tiny spiritual "stomachs" and others have voracious spiritual "hungers." Most of us alternate between the two extremes; sometimes we are famished for righteousness and

at other times we pick at it. (God must despair at our fickleness as much as a mother trying to feed her children.)

Overstress, however, tends to make us completely lose our appetites for God. We no longer feel the desire for communion with him or long to be cleansed in spirit. We become preoccupied with diversions and too fatigued to pray. Sadly, this diminished spiritual energy also robs us of the very resources we need to cope with the stresses of life. Since we abandon the Source of all energy, we are easily beaten by temptation and tribulation.

Just a few weeks ago a patient came to see me who had been struggling to overcome depression. He told me how his illness had depleted his spiritual hunger to the point that he was spiritually "lukewarm," ready to be "spewed out" of God's mouth. So he decided to go away for a weekend by himself and to spend the time in rest and spiritual renewal. Away from his stresses, like Jacob, he wrestled with God— and with himself. And he found that giving time to prayer and meditation (even though he didn't really *feel* like praying) gave him renewed strength. Not only is his depression passing away, but his appetite for God is coming back. All he needed was a retreat from the stress of his life—and God is doing the rest.

(2) *Overstress produces destructive spiritual energy.* Stress can bring out the worst in us! Some of us are not pleasant to be around as it is, but when we are overstressed the Mr. Hyde in *all* of us emerges. We become irritable, moody, angry, and unpleasant, and we release a very negative and destructive spiritual energy. We are less able to resist evil, and we end up causing harm to ourselves and others. Overstress seems to release everything that is bad within us.

A Third Spiritual Consequence of Stress

There is a third, more subtle way overstress can harm us spiritually: (3) *We can begin to confuse adrenalin arousal and true spirituality.*

As I have shown in previous chapters, not all destructive stress is unpleasant. A constant state of adrenalin arousal, although physically damaging, is often experienced as pleasant excitement and stimulation. And it is this that makes it most dangerous, because we can come to think of the aroused state as "normal" and to depend on the high it gives us to get anything accomplished.

I believe there is a corresponding spiritual danger. Becoming dependent on adrenalin arousal for the good feelings of life can create an association between spirituality and high arousal. In other words, one doesn't feel "spiritual" unless one is also being stimulated by adrenalin arousal.

Many expressions of spirituality have become linked to adrenalin arousal, and this can be very harmful. A great many of the true saints of God have found their peak spiritual experiences in quietness and solitude. But many modern "saints" look for it only in exciting challenges or emotional catharsis.

When we were in our early twenties, my wife and I were very friendly with another Christian couple. All four of us longed for and sought a deeper experience of God. My wife and I decided that we would grow spiritually if we settled in one church and tried to be responsible, faithful, and diligent in our Christian witness and service.

The other couple felt the need for more stimulation in order to grow, and were always looking for some new experience. So they moved from church to church. As soon as the preaching of one minister became familiar to them, they no longer felt "moved," so they packed their Bibles and moved on. They did this about every three months, even "recycling" some churches when their memories had faded enough to make the old seem new again.

Round and round these friends of ours went, always looking for some new excitement and challenge. Finally, after three years, they became totally disillusioned, and they gave up on church altogether. They began to look to worldly pleasure to supply the stimulation that regular church attendance no longer gave them.

It was years before I realized what our friends were doing. They had come to confuse adrenalin arousal with spiritual growth. If their bodies were stimulated, they felt they were growing spiritually. If they were not stimulated, they felt nothing was happening.

The saddest thing about this kind of confusion is that it actually works *against* spiritual growth. Why? Because when we confuse adrenalin arousal for spirituality we start to worship our own bodies instead of God! We think we are listening for God's voice when we are actually waiting for our adrenalin system to be aroused. Unless the body is "revved up" there is no hunger for God. Unless there is physical stimulation, there is no desire for righteousness.

We need to learn again the truth of 1 Peter 3:4, which was meant for wives in the original context but is helpful for all of us to remember as a prescription for stress-free living: "Be beautiful inside, in your hearts, with the lasting charm of a gentle and *quiet* spirit which is so precious to God" (LB, italics mine).

Adrenalin and Prayer

I would even go further and say that the state of adrenalin arousal is not conducive to meaningful prayer—they just don't mix that well. Adrenalin arousal speeds us up, while prayer should slow us down. ("Be still and know that I am God," Ps. 46:10.) Most of us move so quickly that we get out of step with God; we can't take time to "be still" and wait for his voice. How on earth is it possible then to converse with him?

This is something many of us have not yet realized. My wife recently took a class on prayer at our seminary. As part of the course of study the class carried out a survey of other students' prayer habits. What they discovered was that 85 percent of the students surveyed (most of them preparing for the professional ministry) said they were so rushed that they only had time to "pray on the run."

Such prayer has become a lifestyle for many Christians. And while "flash" prayers in odd moments can be helpful, a prayer life that consists entirely of praying "on the run" is hardly conducive to spiritual growth.

Some years ago a colleague of mine and I performed an interesting experiment. We wanted to examine the physiological correlates of prayer. We invited a half-dozen people we knew were sincere in their praying to allow us to monitor their bodies while they prayed.

What we found was that most of them created a state of heightened arousal when they prayed—their blood pressure and heart rate went up, their respiration increased, skin temperature went down, and they perspired more. They were obviously praying with their adrenalin. Few had learned to commune with God in a way that was peaceful and quiet.

Now, I have no way of knowing how effective or meaningful the prayers of these students were. And I cannot say it is *wrong* to become excited when we pray. Perhaps it is simply human nature to become keyed up about something as important and meaningful as prayer. But I strongly suspect that much of the arousal these students experienced was more a matter of physical habit than spiritual benefit, and that their prayers would have been just as effective if there had been less arousal. The more I see of the damage elevated adrenalin can do, the less I believe that a loving Lord would want us consistently to endanger our health through the way we talk to him!

At the seminary where I teach, we are now trying to show students how to commune with God without always being "on the run" or always "praying with their adrenalin." My concern is that so many Christians are so accustomed to creating adrenalin arousal as the only way to worship that they don't know how to do it any other way! And I believe it is important to encourage both excitement and peaceful relaxation in our worship exercises.

Should Christians Be Free of Harmful Stress—And Are They?

This brings us back to a very basic question: Should Christians be free of stress? That is not easy to answer. On the one hand, stress is an essential part of life. We must live in the world, and all living produces stress. Being a Christian in a hedonistic and selfish world can be especially stressful.

We saw in earlier chapters that not all stress is bad; a certain amount of it is essential to our well-being. But we also saw that *too much stress*—especially stress that is not relieved by times of rest and renewal—can harm us physically, mentally, and spiritually.

So while I cannot say that a Christian should be totally free of stress, I think I *can* say that Christians should not allow themselves to become so stressed as to produce damage to their bodies, minds, and spirits.

That is not to say it doesn't happen! To a great extent, Christians are caught up in the same rat race as everyone else. We have let our values become distorted and don't see life clearly from God's perspective. We've lost some of our distinctiveness; our lives are almost identical to those of people who are not committed to Christ. As a result, I believe we are violating very basic laws that God has set down for our bodies (the "temple of the Holy Spirit"). And we may be doing this all in the name of One who came to save us from our need to earn salvation!

Christians must wake up to the fact that they are burning themselves out just as quickly as everyone else is! Change is occurring so rapidly and hurry sickness is so rampant in our society that avoiding stress damage takes an extra effort. And the sad fact is that relatively few people—even Christians—are making that extra effort.

Alvin Toffler, who in his book *Future Shock* warned about the effects of rapid change, also commented on this fact. He wrote:

The disturbing fact is that the vast majority of people, including educated and otherwise sophisticated [I would add "God-fearing"] people find the idea of change so threatening that they attempt to deny its existence. Even those people who understand intellectually that change is accelerating have not internalized that knowledge, do not take this critical social fact into account in planning their own personal lives.[1]

In order to be salt and light in today's hurry-sick society, Christians *must learn to cope creatively with change.* I believe God is calling us to be different—to be free of the damaging effects of overstress produced by a world bent on hurrying itself to destruction.

Do you remember what the apostle Paul said to the Thessalonians: "That every one of you should know how to possess his vessel in sanctification and honor" (1 Thess. 4:4)? Another translation renders it this way: "Each one of you must learn to gain mastery over his body" (NEB).

In its original context, this verse had to do with sex, but given the seriousness of the stress problem today and the crisis facing us as Christian people, Paul's words are as appropriate to the problem of stress as they are to lust. We must gain *mastery* over our stress. In the chapters to come I hope to show some practical ways this can be done.

God's Resources for Coping with Stress

There is no better program of stress management than learning how to use the resources for living that God has provided. The gospel is complete in *every* respect and provides us with a powerful prescription for effective living. It provides us with resources for helping us cope with stress so as to avoid the negative physical, emotional, and spiritual consequences that result from overstress. God has made provision for us:

---

1. (New York: Random House, 1970.)

- to live peacefully
- to live productively
- to live efficiently
- to live harmoniously.

By replanning our lives around his values we can learn that "hurry sickness" is not meant to be our inevitable end. We can live peacefully and in harmony with God's purposes.

Remember that Jesus told us: "Seek ye first the kingdom of God, and his righteousness; and all these things shall be added unto you" (Matt. 6:33). My wife and I had this text engraved on the inside of her wedding ring thirty years ago. It is still there, and our experience has been that it holds the key to the healthiest way to live and cope with stress in our lives.

We will never be able completely to avoid stress-producing situations. Some of us may be able to change jobs in order to get away from conflict or move to another neighborhood to avoid the tyranny of stress, but not everybody is free to choose the ideal work or living situation. We can't all live far from freeways, noisy trains, or teenagers playing rock music.

All of us must learn how to build effective filters against stress right where we are. Careful planning and increased awareness of the source of our stress can avoid much stress damage. It is my hope this book will be helpful in showing some specific ways to do this.

But there will always be times when the pain of overstress surrounds us and we can do no more than patiently "face the music." This is where faith in God can transform pain into patient endurance and overstress into peaceful tolerance. The secret is in the loving attitude God can give us.

Yes, we live in an increasingly stress-producing world. There is less stability in our existence, a greater degree of disillusionment, less sense of clear direction, and more insecurity brought about by rapid change in a society that is not sure where it is headed. *Only* faith in a stable, unchanging God can save us from being destroyed by such a world. He is the same yesterday, today, and forever, and believing this truth should have a great influence on our ability to avoid the damaging consequences of the stress all around us.

Phillip Yancey, in his book, *Where Is God When It Hurts,* sums this truth up well:

> He has been there from the beginning, designing a pain system that still, in the midst of a fallen, rebellious world, bears the stamp of His genius and equips us for life on this planet. . . . He has promised supernatural strength to nourish our spirits, even if our physical suffering goes unrelieved. He has joined us. He has bled and cried and suffered. He has dignified for all time those who suffer by sharing their pain.[2]

In later chapters we will further explore the ways in which Christ can nourish our spirits and relieve the suffering our stress causes us.

2. (Wheaton, IL: Zondervan, 1977), p. 182.

PART TWO

Diagnosing
Your Adrenalin Arousal

"Among all my autopsies (and I have performed well over
a thousand), I have never seen a person who died of old age.
In fact, *I do not think anyone has died of old age yet.*
To permit this would be the ideal accomplishment of medical
research. . . . To die of old age would mean that
all the organs of the body had worn out proportionately,
merely by having been used too long. This is never the case.
We invariably die because one vital part has worn out
too early in proportion to the rest of the body. . . .
The lesson seems to be that, as far as man can
regulate his life by voluntary actions,
he should seek to equalize stress throughout his being! . . .
The human body—like the tires on a car,
or the rug on a floor—wears longest when it wears evenly."
—HANS SELYE
The Stress of Life

"Check up on yourselves. Are you really Christians?
Do you pass the test? Do you feel Christ's presence and power
more and more within you? Or are you just pretending
to be Christians when you aren't at all?"
—2 Corinthians 13:5, LB

5

The Symptoms of Distress

Stress *begins* in the mind but *ends* in the body. This is important to remember. There is no such thing as stress *only* being in the mind. In this chapter I want to look at some of the specific physical effects of stress.

The Body's Defense System

The human body (that marvel of God's creation) is designed with an important system to protect us from stress. All living organisms have such a system, but it reaches its highest state of efficiency and intricacy in the human.

There are three components to this protective system:

(1) An *alarm system* designed to sound a warning when something goes wrong. Pain is a part of this system. It tells us when body tissue is being damaged.

(2) An *activating system* designed to prepare us for action in response to the alarm. This is an emergency system triggered and sustained by adrenalin arousal. It prepares us for the "fight or flight" response.

(3) A *recovery system* designed to provide healing, recuperation, and revitalization. It is the neglect of this recovery system that leads to premature heart disease and many of the other painful consequences of stress.

To understand how these systems operate, let us look at a typical stress reaction in a patient I will call Janice. Janice is thirty-two years old. Like so many women today, she is trying to combine a career with parenting. She is married to a businessman, has two sons aged eight and six, and is going to graduate school in order to get a degree in social work.

It is Monday morning and Janice is trying to get the family off to work and school so she can get to her class. She gets up at six in the morning, while her husband, Jim, is still snoozing in bed. While he is sometimes helpful with the boys, Jim just doesn't have a mother's touch when it comes to preparing a school lunch, getting breakfasts down two little mouths, and putting pants on two little bodies the right way round. So Janice leaves him to sleep for a while.

This particular morning is a bad one. Janice worked on a school paper until late the night before and didn't get enough sleep, so she is tired. The boys are noisier than usual and also slower in dressing themselves. Janice gets angry, loses her patience, and yells at them a little. They pay no attention, so she yells louder. "You're going to make us all late this morning!" she yells for the third time.

Jim appears on the scene, still dressed in his pajamas. He tries to help by saying, "Come on, Janice, they're only little boys. It doesn't matter if they are late for school."

"It does matter to me!" Janice screams back.

And then it hits. A sharp, stabbing pain in the back of the neck, a tight band around the head—she can just feel a classic tension headache coming on. She's had it on many Monday mornings before. And she knows it's going to be a painful day.

The pain is Janice's *alarm system*. And it's telling her she is under too much stress. Just like a bell clanging to warn of a fire, the alarm system serves a *very important* function— if you pay attention to it. Unfortunately, most of us don't. We reach for the painkiller to silence the bell and don't pay attention to the fire!

Janice goes to the bathroom. "I'd better take some aspirin right now before this headache gets any worse," she thinks.

She comes back to the kitchen. The boys still aren't ready

to go. "Now that's it; I've had enough! If you boys don't hurry I'm going to punish you." She moves into high gear. In a few quick moves she has everything quickly organized; before the boys know it, they've been bundled into the car and are on their way to school.

This is Janice's *activating system* in action. Her stress has made her more efficient, energized, and action oriented. Her adrenalin is pumping faster than ever. She can move quickly, make snap decisions, and even temporarily suppress her headache. The high level of activity feels good to her. The adrenalin almost gives her a "high." More important, she feels in control again.

Janice drops the boys off at school, races to the university, and gets to class just as the professor is about to begin his lecture. She settles into her chair. Slowly her adrenalin level drops. No more action is needed, just a quiet receiving of knowledge. The headache starts to come back, only more intensely. She feels a flutter in her chest, as if her heart had skipped a beat. Suddenly she feels tired and old—all worn out and listless. She yawns. "I wish I could just go back to bed and sleep the rest of the day," she thinks.

She is now under the control of her *recovery system*. Her adrenalin has let down and her body is demanding time for recuperation. She is in desperate need of rest. Unfortunately, before bedtime there will be many more occasions for her alarm, activation, and recovery systems to be triggered. It's going to be a tough day for Janice.

Cooperate with Your Body

These three reactions—alarm, activation, and recovery— are "automatic." They happen without our having to think about them, and this is why they can cause us so much trouble! Because they happen without our thinking about them we don't always realize how important it is to cooperate with them. (Remember, the entire system is designed to protect us!)

To understand how the protection system functions, fix in your mind the following sequence of reaction to stress:

(1) ALARM ➡ **(2) ACTIVATION** ➡ **(3) RECOVERY**

We can learn to be more aware of where we are in the sequence at any time, and this makes it easier for us to cooperate with it. Let's examine each system separately:

(1) *Alarm.* The purpose of the alarm system is to warn us that our bodies are being pushed beyond their limits. The body is provided with many "pain" signals, all designed to protect us. Unfortunately, in our performance-oriented culture, we've come to believe that pain is an enemy rather than a friend. When we experience pain, we try to remove it, rather than heed the signal. Seldom do we stop and say, "This pain is telling me something; let me pay attention to its message before I take it away."

Janice's headache was a sign that her alarm system was going off loud and clear. She should have slowed down, realized she was under too much pressure, reordered her priorities, asked her husband for help, and "quietened" her hurried heart. This would have made for a more peaceful atmosphere and would have helped her avoid a painful stress experience.

(2) *Activation.* Sometimes, but not always, it is important to move to the activation stage. This occurs when adrenalin is recruited and the "fight or flight" reaction is triggered. As a result, we are mobilized to act; we become physically stronger (which can be dangerous if we are angry) and mentally "sharper." Notice I said "sharper," not "more creative or innovative." When adrenalin is high, we are enabled to be more focused and directed. Snap decisions are easy. Thoughtful decisions are impossible. In the emergency mode, speed is what is required.

Activation is appropriate when the situation warrants it.

Emergencies and other pressing demands require that we act. But we are not designed to stay activated all the time! Sooner or later—and the sooner the better—we must allow the next system to begin operating.

(3) *Recovery.* This is the most misunderstood and neglected system of all. We don't cooperate very well with it because we have been taught to feel guilty whenever we indulge in rest. Also, the lowering level of adrenalin during recovery is invariably accompanied by a feeling of depression. And we just don't like feeling depressed—even when the feeling is a natural part of a healthy stress response.

It is also during the recovery stage that many of the more painful consequences of stress are felt. While our adrenalin is up, we are protected from pain. When it drops we are not, and we begin to feel the negative effects of stress—such as headaches or diarrhea.

The "low" of the recovery state is commonly called the "post-adrenalin blues," and it is not unlike the feeling of anticlimax that we experience after we've had a "mountain-top" experience. Elijah had it after his victory against the prophets of Baal on Mount Carmel. After God's fire had consumed the bullock saturated with water, Elijah fled into the wilderness, sat down under a juniper tree, and wished he might die. He needed recovery and rejuvenation—which is what God then gave him.

Knowing how to cooperate with the recovery stage is the focus of Part 3 of this book, so I won't pursue it any further here except to say: Thank God for your recovery system every time you feel it! If you understand how vitally important it is to a healthy and happy life, you won't feel as bad when the post-adrenalin slump comes. The more you allow yourself to "let down," the quicker your recovery will be.

If You Don't Cooperate

What if you do not heed the alarm system, limit the workings of the activating system, or cooperate with the recovery system? There is only one answer: You develop stress disease! But it is fascinating to note that each person seems to experience stress disease differently. It seems as if we each have our "weak spot."

A chain of many links, even though it has been very carefully made, almost always has one link that is weaker than the others. When the chain is subjected to strain, this one weak link will snap before the others. In the same way, each of us, partly because of the genes we've inherited and partly because of the ways we've learned to react to stress, will show our stress response in a unique way. Before we explore some of these different ways, I suggest that you take a moment to write down some notes about your own unique way of experiencing stress. You will find the next section more beneficial if you ask yourself: What is the first symptom I feel when I am stressed? How does this symptom start? When does it begin? Does it move from one part of my body to another? How long does it last? See if you can recognize the sequence of alarm, activation, and recovery in each experience of extreme stress you have had.

The Symptoms of Distress

In chapters 1 and 2 we examined how stress generally affects the body. Now we will look more specifically at the variety of symptoms that accompany stress disease.

Let me caution you to be very careful at this point. While it is my intention to increase your awareness of stress disease and help you recognize stress symptoms, it is very easy to misread verbal descriptions and either exaggerate the severity of minor symptoms or minimize the importance of major ones. Consult a physician or psychologist if you are at all concerned about any of these symptoms.

Figure 3 summarizes the effects of stress on various parts of the body. Examine the figure so as to understand the change occurring in each organ, then read the following list of symptoms associated with those organs.

(1) *Brain:* generalized panic and anxiety, migraine headaches

(2) *Heart:* rapid heartbeat, skipped beats, raised blood pressure, thumping and mid-sternum mild pain; dizziness and light headedness from high blood pressure, palpitations

(3) *Stomach and Intestines:* general gastric distress, feelings of nausea, acid stomach and heartburn, diarrhea (chronic and acute), some forms of colitis, indigestion, constipation, churning

(4) *Muscles:* neck ache and shoulder pain, headaches, stiff neck, teeth grinding, jaw joint pain (transmandibular joint syndrome); high and low back pain; generalized pain in arms and legs

(5) *Hands and Skin:* cold extremities, increased sweating, skin eruptions

(6) *Lungs:* respiratory problems, some asthmas, hyperventilation syndrome, shortness of breath

(7) *General:* feelings of "trembling," fear of impending doom, inability to sit long, squirming and fidgetiness, foot tapping, pacing, feelings of fatigue and lack of energy or heaviness, heightened irritability and anger, racing thoughts, daydreaming, indecisiveness, sleep disruption

Which are the more common symptoms of overstress? An interesting study by Drs. Jonathan C. Smith and Jeffrey M. Seidel of Roosevelt University[1] examined the symptoms reported by more than twelve hundred subjects and broke them down into "factors"—Smith and Seidel found eighteen interpretable factors. The most notable was gastric distress, followed by disturbed cardiorespiratory activity, restless activity, self-conscious activity, feelings of fatigue and lack of energy, and headaches. Other factors included backache; skin difficulties; shoulder, neck, and back tension; and trembling and shaking. Of all these factors, gastric distress was

---

1. Published in *Biofeedback and Self-Regulation,* vol. 7, no. 1, 1982.

FIGURE 3
The Effects of Stress on the Body

**Perceived Challenge
or Threat**

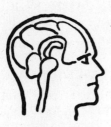

**Brain: Increased blood flow
Awake and alert**

**Heart: Increased heart rate
Elevated blood pressure**

**Stomach: Secretion of extra acid
Accelerated digestion**

**Muscles: Extra blood supply
Increased tension**

**Lungs: Increased level of oxygen in
blood
Removal of waste gas**

**Skin: Sweating increases
Blood is withdrawn from
extremities (hands become
cold)**

the greatest, being four times more common than the next highest. This complaint included stomach discomfort, pain, excess secretion of acid, and churning. There was no difference in frequency of occurrence between males and females.

This is a formidable list of symptoms! And since many of them can also be caused by problems other than stress, it usually takes a professionally trained person to make a careful differential diagnosis. It's a good idea to seek professional help if you are bothered by any of these symptoms.

It is possible, however, to use the symptoms described above to gain a general picture of the level of stress in your life. Figure 4 presents a simple objective test to help you do this. The instructions are simple: Think back over your life during the past several months. Then read through the list of symptoms, asking yourself whether any of them have been a bother to you. Rate the intensity of the symptom according to the scale listed with the chart and write the appropriate number under "Rating." When you have finished, add up your "score" and compare it to the chart in Appendix 1. The total score will be somewhere between zero and sixty. The higher the score, the greater your level of distress.

Obviously, a test like this is subject to distortion by either exaggerating your symptoms or undervaluing them. If you don't trust your judgment, then ask a close and trusted friend to go over the test with you. In dialogue with this friend you might just be more accurate. And once again, do not hesitate to seek professional help.

Remember, also, that even though your score may not be very high, you might still be heading for one of the "hidden" forms of stress disease! Very often the excitement of high adrenalin arousal can mask the insidious damage going on in the heart, vascular system, or stomach. High adrenalin often masks pain, and habitually aroused people can sometimes avoid all the symptoms of distress until stress disease is very far advanced.

FIGURE 4
Symptoms of Distress

Answer the questions listed below according to the following scale:

Rating	Description
0	I do not experience this symptom at all.
1	I sometimes (perhaps once a month) experience this symptom.
2	I experience this symptom more than once a month, but not more than once a week.
3	I experience this symptom often (more than once a week).

	SYMPTOM	RATING
1	1. Do you experience headaches of any sort?	1
3	2. Do you experience tension or stiffness in your neck, shoulders, jaw, arms, hands, legs, or stomach?	1
3	3. Do you have nervous tics, or do you tremble?	1
2	4. Do you feel your heart thumping or racing?	1
0	5. Do you get irregular heartbeats, or does your heart skip beats?	1
0	6. Do you have difficulty breathing at times?	3
0	7. Do you ever get dizzy or lightheaded?	1
0	8. Do you feel as though you have a lump in your throat or you have to clear it?	1
1	9. Do you suffer from colds, the flu, or hoarseness?	0
1	10. Are you bothered by indigestion, nausea, or discomfort in your stomach?	3
0	11. Do you have diarrhea or constipation?	2
0	12. Do you bite your nails?	0
1	13. Do you have difficulty falling or staying asleep?	0
1	14. Do you wake up feeling tired?	1
3	15. Are your hands or feet cold?	2
3	16. Do you grind or grit your teeth, or do your jaws ache?	3
0	17. Are you prone to excess perspiration?	1
3	18. Are you angry or irritable?	3
1	19. Do you feel a lot of generalized pain (back pain, stomach pain, head pain, muscle pain, etc.)?	2
3	20. Have you become aware of increased anxiety, worry, fidgitiness, or restlessness?	3

26

Headaches and Distress

While different people show their distress in different ways, a very important indicator that stress is out of control in most people is a *headache*.

There are many types of headaches (at least fifteen categories are recognized), not all of them are stress-related. But the most common form of headache is the kind known variously as tension headache, muscle contraction headache, or stress headache, and such headaches afflict between fifty and a hundred million people in the United States.

Because migraine headaches are also quite common, let me point out that there are important differences between migraines and tension headaches. But the two are often confused because many people who actually have tension headaches prefer to be known as "migraine" sufferers (there is less stigma, I suppose). And the picture is further complicated by the fact that both migraines and tension headaches can be stress-related.

Migraines are typically felt in one side of the head and often involve nausea or vomiting. The pain is sharp and throbbing. Migraines can come on at any time, even waking the sufferer in the middle of the night.

Tension headaches, on the other hand, are dull and "pressured." They come on during the day, and sleep helps to relieve them. The pain can be at the back of, front of, or over the whole head. Often it feels like a tight band or a squeezing from all sides, because it is really the muscles of the face and head that are causing the pain.

Sometimes the pain comes from the joints in the jaw and sometimes from the muscles in the temple area. The inability to open the mouth wide enough to accept three fingers vertically is sometimes taken as a sign of reduced jaw joint mobility. Another sign is a popping or cracking sound as the mouth is opened or closed. Since this sometimes can be related to stress, professional help should be sought for it as soon as possible.

Tension headaches can be caused by stress in a number of ways. First, the sustained higher muscle tension produced by adrenalin and neural triggering can create pain because the muscle fibers become fatigued. Second, the heightened tension releases pain-producing chemicals into the muscle fibers. Third, there can be a reduction of blood supply to these muscles, presumably because the blood is needed by those muscles used to fight or flee. The muscles involved in tension headaches are not needed for any such emergency function.

Migraine headaches (and there are many varieties) are due to inflammation and contraction of blood vessels in the head and brain. The predisposition to migraines is mostly inherited, but stress can trigger migraine headaches in susceptible persons causing an increase in the blood flow to the brain (started by the action of the adrenalin). The hands often get cold just before a migraine attack because the blood is being shunted elsewhere, and migraine sufferers also tend to have chronic cold hands and feet.

Cluster headaches (a variation of migraine) are much less common than either tension or classic migraine headaches. They are called "clusters" because they come in groups, occurring once or several times a day for a few days, then going away. The pain is very severe, and men suffer from it five times more often than women. Whether or not cluster headaches can be triggered or aggravated by stress is not clear, although I suspect they are much less stress-related than either tension or migraine headaches.

Diseases of the eyes, ears, nose, or bones of the skull and neck can cause head pain, as can infections and tumors. A physician can readily diagnose these. Obviously, these are not stress-related. But more subtle headaches can come from environmental conditions or foods, and these can, to a certain degree, be connected to stress.

Foods that cause headaches in some people include egg whites, caffeine, ice cream, sugar, and hot dogs. Just how these foods trigger headaches and whether stress aggravates them is not known. Presumably there is some allergic or other reaction that is very specific to the affected person. I know, for instance, that strong fluorescent lights, such as those found in supermarkets and the like, trigger a headache in me. When I am under stress, the headaches seem worse. The same is true for prolonged working under such lights. I suspect that I have some marked sensitivity to the rapid flashing produced by these lights in contrast to incandescent lights and that this becomes a "stressor" to my body.

Allergies and Stress

Allergies, in general, can produce headaches as well as myriad other reactions such as hay fever, asthma, gastrointestinal disturbance, hives, and behavior problems. An allergic substance is anything that alters the reaction of tissues in some people while being innocuous to others. If everyone suffered the same reaction it would be called a "poison." Because it affects only some people, it is called an allergen. (For the sufferer, it is a poison nevertheless.)

I am very allergic to the fine fur on the skin of peaches. I break out in an itching rash that nothing can soothe. The effect is *immediate.* Other types of allergens have a *delayed* effect.

To what extent is an allergic reaction or allergic headache stress-related? We have no proof at this point, but there is abundant anecdotal evidence that when someone is highly stressed, any allergic predisposition may be greatly aggravated. So while stress may not be the *cause* of the allergy, it could certainly be a *trigger.* Reducing one's stress level can therefore reduce the frequency with which an allergic reaction is experienced.

Effects of Chronic Stress

There are three more generalized effects of stress I would like to mention because they can account for so many of

the ailments we suffer today. An understanding of them can
be very helpful in recognizing stress.

When stress is chronic—that is, when it is continuous and
doesn't let up or allow the body adequate time for recovery,
the following happens:

(1) *The immune system becomes depleted.* The immune
system is that part of the body designed to fight off disease
and infection. Certain hormones, white blood cells, and a
host of other complex mechanisms are designed to fight off
all intruders in body tissue. There are even a few hormones
that help facilitate how the body combats disease under conditions of stress. But when the total system is under duress,
as it is when stress is chronic, something must be sacrificed
in order to protect the body as a whole. The immune system
then becomes depleted.

What is the consequence of this? Under prolonged stress
we tend to become sick more often. Infections get us; the
flu strikes when we don't expect it. And the body does not
heal as rapidly as it does in times of less stress.

There is even strong evidence that certain cancers grow
more rapidly under stressful conditions. And it is suspected
that other disorders such as rheumatoid arthritis are caused
or at least aggravated by stress. Life events such as separation
from a loved one, marital difficulties, or general emotional
strain all seem to be aggravating factors in much disease
because they produce stress.

(2) *The anti-pain system becomes depleted.* This is another
unexpected (but not unexplainable) reaction to prolonged
stress. In recent years it has been discovered that the brain
has its own analgesics circulating within. These are pain-
killing hormones called "endorphins" (short for endogenous
morphine) that are as powerful as morphine. These brain
hormones help to control pain.

During some forms of stress, especially the short-lived,
acute forms, the body may produce more endorphin, and
this helps to switch off our pain signals. Elevated adrenalin,
however, can block pain in another way.

For instance, if you were caught in an emergency, you would have remarkable strength and pain control. Let's imagine you are camping in the mountains with a friend. While you are out hiking one day, your friend falls and is seriously injured. The only way to get help is to run three or four miles to the nearest ranger station. During such an emergency, you may find you are able to run the distance extra-fast and feel no pain at all from the thorns you tramp on or the toes you stub. This is because your body "ignores" pain during times of heightened arousal. It focuses on the emergency needs and your brain blocks out other signals.

But we do not see the same pain-killing reaction in cases of chronic stress. When the demand is unrelenting, day in and day out, the endorphins become depleted. Awareness of pain increases and tolerance for discomfort decreases. This is one of the reasons why stress-related illnesses are so often linked to feelings of pain all over the body.

(3) *The anti-anxiety system becomes depleted.* Just as the brain has endorphins to inhibit pain, it also has its own tranquilizers to inhibit anxiety. Under prolonged conditions of stress, however, these natural tranquilizers become depleted and the experience of anxiety goes up. This can make us prone to panic attacks. The mind becomes obsessed with petty problems and thoughts keep going round and round like a stuck record.

Medication Isn't the Answer

These three adverse effects of chronic stress—reduced immune defense, increased pain, and increased anxiety—are common in our hurried-up culture. And while we have developed a variety of chemical weapons (medication) to help protect us from them, including antibiotics to make up for the depleted immune system, analgesics to kill pain, and tranquilizers to take away anxiety, we are still not dealing adequately with the source of the problem.

These three types of medication, together with antacids

to dilute stomach acids, are the most commonly consumed medicines today. Vast quantities are prescribed by almost every physician in practice. Unfortunately, they all give testimony to the fact that we are a stress-riddled society.

Actually, the physical consequences of stress can have a positive side if we see them as warning signals and heed their messages. If you think about it, they are all designed to protect us. The increased proneness to illness, the extra pain, and the restless anxiety should cause us to pull back and disengage from our stress. They are telling us we are overdoing things and even helping us to find a solution.

Since realizing that my body is intelligently designed I have changed my attitude to the symptoms of distress that I experience from time to time. I now try to remember to thank God when I get sick with the flu. I praise him when I feel pain and I glorify him when I am anxious. I have been able to see all of these as God's gifts to me, designed to help me balance my life a little better and place all the demands clamoring for my attention under his control. By cooperating with my discomfort and not rushing to take it away with a pill, I allow God to heal me wholly—not just the physical symptom, but also the attitude—the hurry—that is the cause of my stress.

6

Are You
An Adrenalin Addict?

Every day around four in the afternoon Terrence begins to feel restless. He gets edgy, fidgets at the lathe which is his responsibility at work, and begins watching the clock. That last hour passes as slowly as eternity. It's time for his "fix" and he can't wait for the clock to strike five so he can leave work and head for the track.

You see, Terrence is hooked on running. He runs at least five miles a day, sometimes ten. And when too much time elapses between his last run and the next he gets "antsy."

"I knew I was a running junkie when I realized I structured my whole life around my time at the track. I do it for the 'high' it gives me. There is something exhilarating about running. And it's better than spending time in a bar drinking beer," Terrence says proudly.

The Addictive Urge

Terrence is not alone in his dependency. Literally thousands of us are hooked on some activity or interest, just as an alcoholic is addicted to alcohol, and we depend on that activity for the "kick" it gives us. We may have either a psychological dependence or a physiological addiction to the chemistry involved—or both. Whatever the underlying reasons, the result is that we don't feel normal unless we're doing the activity!

A friend of mine, for instance, is hooked on mountain climbing. Ever since he can remember he has longed to be on the peak of some mountain. "When I get to the top I feel ecstatic," he will tell you joyfully.

A client of mine is a "chocoholic" and another is hooked on collecting bottle tops. I'm beginning to think my wife is hooked on crocheting. Every free moment she has is given to nimble fingering of a plastic stick with a hook on the end that goes in and out of deftly formed loops. "Why do you do it?" I ask her. "Because I enjoy it," she profoundly replies. Who can argue with that?

While many of these activities are simply psychological outlets for tension or anxiety, some reinforce a dependency because they produce a high level of pleasure and a feeling of need or deprivation when they are removed.

But can we really compare an ice cream or running "habit" with alcoholism or drug addiction? Of course, there are obvious and important differences, as indicated by the different terminology used to denote different kinds of habits. "Dependency" usually refers only to psychological needs, although who knows what complex body chemistry underlies our pleasure centers? "Addiction" technically refers to physical needs—a chemical dependency that can produce extreme physical discomfort when the body is deprived of the addictive substance.

But in some ways all these habits are very much alike, because underlying all these conditions is the human tendency to get "hooked" on activities that give us intense pleasure—whether the pleasure is psychological or physiological. Many experts are now saying that almost *any* activity can become "addicting" (and here I suspect they are referring to both dependency and addiction), although some activities produce stronger attachments than others and some of us are more prone to becoming hooked on certain activities (depending on our personality, the nature of the activity, and many other factors).

Eating, sleeping, walking, riding, sex, hobbies, TV watching, smoking, video games, gossip—all have the ability to hook us. Even fishing, which produces in some a profound state of relaxation, can be habit-forming. Both stimulating and tranquilizing activities can create dependency, even though they produce opposite effects.

Is this necessarily bad? No, obviously not—at least not always. Most of the activities I have listed are essentially harmless. And some—such as exercise and sleep—are in themselves beneficial. Who could complain about being addicted to sleep? And Terrence is probably right that running is better for him than spending the equivalent amount of time in a bar.

But the trouble with any kind of dependent or addictive behavior is that people can come to use it as a form of escape to help them cope with problems and to relieve anxiety. This can cause them to rely on the activity too heavily and to run away from the underlying cause of the problem. Also, people who become addicted to an activity or experience will suffer physical and/or emotional "withdrawal" when they can't get their "fix," especially if there is some complex body chemistry involved in the activity. The truth is we don't fully understand how the body experiences pleasure.

Research being done at a number of universities is beginning to show that the mechanisms underlying dependency on activities and interests (previously thought to be purely psychological) may actually be very similar to those involving drugs and alcohol addiction or cigarette smoking.

"There are biological, psychological, and sociological common denominators between drug abuse and other habitual behaviors," says psychologist Dr. Harvey Milkman of Metropolitan State College in Denver. "You are addicted if you cannot control when you start or stop an activity." In this respect all addictions are alike—they can rob us of control over our lives.

Addicted to Adrenalin?

I believe that dependency on certain "exciting" activities, hobbies, and challenges has another feature in common with well-known addictions such as alcoholism or drug abuse.

They are *also* drug addictions—only the drug is from *within,* not outside, the body.

What I mean is that *it is actually possible for us to become addicted to our own adrenalin!* We can get hooked on the pleasurable "high" that comes from the workings of the body's defense system. Both psychological dependency on the excitement of adrenalin arousal as well as physical addiction to the hormone can be involved. And this can be a powerful controller of our actions and emotions.

The addiction starts when the body produces large amounts of adrenalin and related hormones under conditions of stress. As we have seen in previous chapters, this adrenalin creates a surge of energy to help the body respond to the stressful challenge. And as we have also seen, this surge of activity often feels good! Pain is suppressed and we feel excited and powerful.

Because the adrenalin response can be intensely pleasurable, however, and human beings have a tendency to become dependent on anything pleasurable, it is possible for us to actually become hooked on the "adrenalin high" to the point that we crave it over and over. We learn to "psych" ourselves up to a high level of adrenalin arousal with certain actions and attitudes just to feel good. And the danger is that we can become dependent on the body's emergency system to carry out our normal, everyday lives. When we are deprived of the adrenalin high we suffer from "withdrawal"—a "post-adrenalin depression."

Obviously, the chemicals of the body that can cause the addiction to adrenalin are many and complex. And there are undoubtedly psychological as well as physiological factors at work in any addiction. My purpose here is not to give a lesson in either biochemistry or psychology. But I believe there is no other way that we can fully account for why we derive as much pleasure from certain activities as from alcohol, as much excitement from interesting tasks as from drugs. It is logical to assume that the body's "pleasure centers" are being stimulated by its own internal chemistry as well as by the psychological pleasure the person experiences.

I believe it is impossible to separate the brain's activities from the underlying biochemistry that causes the brain's activity.

The idea of adrenalin addiction has important implications for how we respond to stress, because the very adrenalin that gives us "kicks" is also the drug that causes us distress when used to excess. And we all have the potential to become dependent, if not addicted, to it. If we do not learn to "back off" from our adrenalin "highs," the very pleasure we derive from even basically healthy endeavors can be a slow form of self-destruction.

Many Christian believers would be shocked to discover they were hooked on their own adrenalin. They abhor the idea that some medication or artificial stimulant would have them bound in its clutches. Yet they are oblivious to a dangerous addiction that can develop without their even being aware of it.

How do you know when you are addicted to your own adrenalin? A good sign is having one or more of the following reactions concerning a specific activity:

- You would rather engage in your activity than sleep.
- When you stop your activity you feel very unhappy.
- You only feel excited or encouraged when you engage in your activity; at other times you feel "low."
- Your activity helps you forget your problems.
- Whenever you feel depressed, you turn to your activity to make you feel better.
- You fantasize a lot about your activity when you are away from it.

The more you can answer "yes" to the above statements, the greater is the likelihood that you are "hooked" on the adrenalin high that activity gives you.

Workaholism As Adrenalin Addiction

It is especially easy for many of us to get hooked on the challenges of a job or career, because attachment to work is so highly valued in our work-centered culture. While "workaholism" can sometimes mask home problems or basic insecurities, most often it is an addiction to the adrenalin surges brought on by challenge and competition.

Competition is as part of the American way of life as apple pie and baseball. Schools and businesses depend on and utilize the "high" that a challenge can create. They know how to open the floodgates and cause vast quantities of adrenalin to be released into the bloodstream by capitalizing on the feeling of exhilaration that adrenalin can bring.

But there is a black lining to this euphoric cloud. What we are doing, says Stanley Sunderwirth, a prominent biochemist, is "drugging ourselves" into an artificial existence. "The addicting activity produces changes in the brain that are the same as or similar to changes produced by drugs. The effect is pleasure—a high." [1] The adrenalin activity that we depend on to help us work long hours and "go the extra mile" for our work produces chemical changes in the brain (and possibly other parts of the body also) that are similar to the changes produced by drugs. The short-term effect is pleasure—but the long-term effect may well be stress disease!

Withdrawal Symptoms of Adrenalin Addiction

Just like any drug addiction, adrenalin addiction involves withdrawal symptoms whenever the body is deprived of the adrenalin.

Only a few months ago, my wife and I went to Hawaii. I was to teach a two-week course to a group of ministers as part of our Doctor of Ministry program. And I decided to take an extra week and have a short vacation before I began to teach.

My wife reports that for the first three days of our vacation I was extremely restless when we were not out sightseeing. Not having anything "to do," I paced around the hotel room

---

1. Quoted from a speech given at a conference on addiction at Denver, Colorado, 1983.

a lot. I sat down for a while, got up, walked to the window, stared at the ocean. I switched on the TV, picked up a book, put it down, and said I was going for a walk. I walked down the seven flights of stairs, looked at a few shop windows, then took the elevator back to the room. I was restless and fidgety. In short, I was experiencing adrenalin withdrawal.

Fortunately, I understood the nature of what I was going through, so I did my best to cooperate with what my body was doing and to go "cold turkey" on adrenalin withdrawal. And it worked! By the fourth day I began to calm down. I felt more relaxed and at peace. My sleeping got better and I became more patient. By the end of the week, I was a normal person again.

It is not uncommon for people to suffer from such withdrawal symptoms during the early part of a vacation. What does this say? I think it says that a lot of us are adrenalin addicts to some extent. This is especially true of those who are Type A, because we produce more adrenalin in the first place!

The signs of adrenalin withdrawal are easy to recognize:
- a strong compulsion to be "doing something" while at home or vacation
- an obsession with thoughts about "what was left undone"
- a feeling of vague guilt while resting
- fidgetiness, restlessness, pacing, leg kicking, or fast gum chewing
- an inability to concentrate for very long on any relaxing activity
- feelings of irritability and aggravation
- a vague (or sometimes profound) feeling of depression whenever you stop an activity.

Adrenal Fatigue

One of the purposes of the stress response is to say to the body, "Prepare for lots of action; get the fuel level up."

The stress hormones are powerful mediators in the conversion of stored sugar into energy. Stored sugar, known as "glycogen" has to be converted to glucose before the body can use it. In response to a demand, the body uses its marvelous intelligence to decide how much glucose is needed. Adrenalin and the related hormones then act as the stimulating signals for the conversion.

Adrenalin also contracts the muscular layer in the walls of the arteries. This, together with speeded-up heart rate, raises the blood pressure and stimulates increased respiration. The extra oxygen, carried in the blood, is needed for increased muscle activity.

Normally, what goes up must come down. As we saw in the previous chapter, the level of adrenalin drops as the demand passes. At this time we normally experience the symptoms of discomfort or distress that come with the wear-and-tear of stress on the body's systems. While adrenalin is elevated, the body seems to be able to fight off disease and discomfort. When it drops, the body tries to return all its systems to a normal level of arousal. It is then that headaches, diarrhea, fatigue, illness, rapid heartbeats, skipped beats, depression, and generalized anxiety are felt. And again, this is part of the normal process of recovery from stress.

However, when the adrenalin level remains high for an extended period of time, a state of "hypoadrenia" or adrenal fatigue can set in. The prolonged state of stress causes the adrenal cortex or outer layer of the adrenal gland to become enlarged, important lymph nodes to shrink, and the stomach and intestines to become irritated. The adrenalin system eventually "crashes" and forces the victim into a state of prolonged and severe fatigue.

Frank is typical of someone suffering from adrenal fatigue. A mechanical engineer who works for a large manufacturing company, he was placed in charge of a new factory and told, "We are way behind in our production schedule; you must do everything possible to get us back on target."

At first, Frank loved the challenge; it brought out the best in him. He saw problems as challenges to be fought and conflicts as tournaments to be won. He started to work longer hours because he couldn't accomplish everything in a normal day. He would often spend whole nights on the job, creating a makeshift bedroom in his office. His wife complained a little, but Frank seemed so happy in his work that she felt guilty for wanting him to come home every night, especially since the factory was a long drive from their home.

No matter how hard Frank worked and whatever progress he made, his superiors demanded more. If he achieved a 5 percent increase in productivity one week, his supervisor at the head office asked for 10 percent the next.

Then suddenly one day everything crashed for Frank. Walking back to his office late in the afternoon, he began to panic. An intense feeling of fear and impending doom overtook him; he began to tremble and could not stand up. So he sat down on a low wall, thinking, "What is happening to me?" Then he felt a great wave of tiredness wash over him. He even thought, "How marvelous it would be to lie down and stop living!"

A colleague found Frank and called the paramedics. He was rushed to the emergency room of the local hospital, where he was diagnosed as suffering from extreme adrenalin fatigue brought on by too much stress. His symptoms were those of a fairly classic anxiety panic attack. This doesn't always show up on tests for adrenal functioning because the values for "normal" range so widely, but it shows itself quite clearly in the victim's sudden inability to tolerate any stress or raise any energy.

For Frank it has been a long struggle back to health. The fatigue limited his activity—including physical activity—for many months. Any kind of exertion, including mild exercise, would increase the lactate level in his blood and send him into another severe panic attack, with strange body sensations and fears.

Now, one-and-a-half years later, Frank is almost his old self again—except that I hope through my therapy with him that he has learned to live a more balanced life. He assures me that he does stop to smell his roses and listen to the birds in his garden as often as possible. He never knew before that birds lived at his house!

Any of the following symptoms should be taken as a sign of impending adrenalin exhaustion:

- intense depression of short duration (say, three days to one week) that occurs every few months
- unusual difficulty in getting energy going in the morning
- being overcome by great tiredness whenever energy is "let down"
- strange body sensations (tingling up and down the arms or across the chest) or strange aches in the joints and muscles
- exhaustion that occurs very easily or frequently
- feelings of panic triggered by activity or exercise.

Mild Forms of Stress Fatigue

Most of us, I suspect, get caught up in crazy work schedules or unreasonable work demands from time to time. But most of us don't experience the dramatic form of stress exhaustion Frank went through (although such an experience is certainly possible for all of us under conditions of extreme and prolonged stress).

Much more common is a milder form of adrenalin fatigue which, while not as serious as the kind of major attack Frank suffered, can nevertheless have a significant negative impact on the quality of our lives.

What are some of the milder and less serious consequences of moderate stress fatigue?

- chronic muscle tension resulting in sore neck, shoulders, and back, as well as in common tension headaches
- disturbance of the digestive system resulting in chronic diarrhea, colitis, diverticulitis, ulcers, or constipation
- chronic sleeplessness, including difficulty falling asleep or waking up very early

- persistent fatigue—especially waking up tired in the morning
- loss of enthusiasm for life, lack of excitement or interest in normal activities
- spiritual lethargy—for Christians, a feeling of boredom with church, other Christians, and even God.

The Cure for Adrenal Fatigue

The remedy for all forms of adrenal fatigue, as we will see shortly, is learning how to manage our arousal so as to allow for adequate recovery time after periods of arousal. This of course means learning to control our addiction to adrenalin, because addiction causes us to crave the "high" of an adrenalin surge just when we should be letting our adrenalin levels drop.

By carefully attending to the symptoms of addiction and fatigue and by heeding the warning inherent in all of them, we can turn our bad stress into good. Learned relaxation, improved sleeping habits, and attention to our spiritual development will aid us in this quest for a balanced life. In the remainder of this book we will be looking at specific techniques for doing this.

Sexual Addiction

In closing this chapter on the addictive tendency in general and adrenalin addiction in particular, I feel constrained to say something about sex as an addictive activity.

Can a person become addicted to sex? Very much so, according to a recent study. Patrick Carnes, a psychologist in Minnesota, has detailed this possibility in a book entitled *The Sexual Addiction*. His very convincing thesis is that some people who seem obsessed with sex show all the classic signs of addiction.

Sex addicts, both men and women, lose control of their libidos. At first they seek acceptable outlets for their cravings, then move to less acceptable ones—frequenting sexually provocative places, having extramarital affairs, employing prostitutes. Finally, some of these people may turn to getting their sexual kicks in bizarre and cruel ways—even to the extreme of associating sex with pain and murder.

What is the underlying addictive mechanism? No doubt there are important psychological factors, but I am strongly convinced that a significant part of the addictive process in such cases is the pairing of high levels of adrenal arousal with the sex drive.

In other words, I believe sex addiction can actually be a form of adrenalin addiction! And the search for higher and higher levels of sexual excitement means that we distort our normal sexuality.

People who confuse sex with adrenalin arousal eventually find that sex is not very satisfying *unless* it is accompanied by the "high" of intense adrenalin arousal. This is one reason so many people find having sex in strange places or with strange partners to be more exciting; they have paired their sexual response with an adrenalin "high." It can even account for why many of the perversions of sex are indulged in by otherwise normal people. Human nature is such that it is always looking for some new kick, and this is true of sex as well as other forms of human activity.

What should a person do if he or she is caught up in such a cycle of response? I believe we must relearn how to be content with the simple hormones and normal arousal of the sexual system, to resist the tendency to seek higher and higher levels of excitement in our sex lives. A person who struggles with this without showing progress should probably consult a professional psychologist or counselor. There may be more deeply seated problems that need to be resolved.

I am sure the apostle Paul also had this in mind when he wrote, "Let me say this, then, speaking for the Lord: Live no longer as the unsaved do, for they are blinded and confused. . . . They don't care anymore about right and wrong and have given themselves over to impure ways. They stop at nothing, being driven by their evil minds and reckless lusts" (Eph. 4:17–19, LB).

When we get our sexual needs mixed up with adrenalin arousal, the potential for sin is very great. The sex drive is powerful enough as it is, but when paired with an addicting hormone it can create a craving for satisfaction that is beyond the point of control for normal persons. This is an addiction— a craving that controls us instead of being controlled by us.

Unfortunately, many sex therapists do not realize how they aggravate the addictive potential of sex by recommending an ever-increasing search for new pleasure. "Why don't you watch porn movies?" or "Increase your fantasy life" are common recommendations from sex therapists. What I believe they should be teaching their patients instead is how to separate their body's defense system (which produces adrenalin arousal) from their sexual response system.

There is much about sexuality in our culture that is inherently neurotic. When fed by an intense need for ever-greater pleasure, it leads down a road of distortion that ultimately destroys the most beautiful relationship outside that between a person and God—the relationship between husband and wife. I am convinced that many marriages would be saved from divorce if only we could get our sexuality back to normal and detach it from a dependence on adrenalin arousal. But that is a topic for another book, still in the gestation stage. At this point I simply want to point out some of the dangers of abusing physical systems that were originally created for our good.

7

Adrenalin and Cholesterol

No discussion about adrenalin and stress disease, especially how they affect the cardiovascular system, would be complete without addressing the question of cholesterol. Report after report in both the popular and professional literature has blamed cholesterol for the rampaging coronary artery disease of our day. But these reports almost totally ignore the role of adrenalin arousal. Consequently, millions of Americans are being deluded into thinking that if their cholesterol level is within certain "normal" limits they are safe from a potential heart attack.

But think again! The game of cardiovascular damage is played by both adrenalin and cholesterol, and the problem cannot be solved by paying attention to only one of the two.

The risk factors for heart disease most commonly highlighted in the popular press are cigarette smoking, high blood pressure, high blood cholesterol levels, diabetes, lack of exercise, obesity, and stress. But while such a list gives some recognition to the stress factor, the use of the term *stress* almost always denotes trauma, tension, or anxiety—the unpleasant or catastrophic aspects of life. If you get fired from your job, you're considered to be under stress. If you are going through a divorce, the stress level is obvious. But as I have already shown, stress is not confined to the painful aspects of life. It is very much a part of *every* demand or arousal—pleasant or unpleasant. And the role this kind of stress plays in causing heart disease depends on cholesterol level.

Simply put, if blood cholesterol levels are high, stress will much more likely contribute to heart disease. On the other hand, if stress levels are kept low, even a high cholesterol level will probably not result in heart disease.

You see, adrenalin and cholesterol work in mutual dependency. The one depends on the other to do the damage of depositing fatty plaque in the arteries. And one without the other is relatively harmless as far as your heart is concerned. But the two together can be deadly.

Of course, there are other factors that can contribute to heart disease as well, so I'm not suggesting a simple one-to-one relationship. But the fact remains that the combination of prolonged adrenalin elevation and high cholesterol is a dangerous one as far as the heart and arteries are concerned.

Understanding Cholesterol

But what is cholesterol, anyway? Is it a poison? Should it be totally eliminated from our bodies?

Although it has the connotation of being something harmful, cholesterol, like adrenalin, has a positive function in our bodies. In fact, it is indispensable for the maintenance of the body. Its main function is to contribute to the building up of cell membranes. It also serves as the basis for bile acids in the liver and for certain hormones. Eighty to 90 percent of the body's total cholesterol is manufactured by the liver. The rest we get from the foods we eat.

Cholesterol is a soapy substance not soluble in water. To become soluble, so as to circulate through the bloodstream, it connects up with protein molecules to form compounds called "lipoproteins." There are *two* different forms of lipoproteins with different ratios of protein to cholesterol. They are high-density lipoproteins (called simply HDLs) and low-density ones (LDLs).

When a doctor gives you your "cholesterol level," he usually is referring to the total blood cholesterol level. But this number tells you nothing about the relative amounts of

HDLs and LDLs. And the difference is crucial, because research has shown that LDLs tend to *increase* the risk for heart disease, while HDLs *lower* the risk.

One other thing research has indicated is that higher circulating adrenalin seems to increase the amount of LDLs in the bloodstream—and therein lies part of the dangerous connection between adrenalin and cholesterol.

Lowering Cholesterol Does Help!

For about twenty-five years now a debate has raged over whether or not lowering cholesterol levels really helps lower the risk of heart and artery disease. I believe the issue has now finally been settled. In January of 1984, the National Health, Lung, and Blood Institute released the findings of a ten-year, $150 million study of the incidence of heart disease among 3,806 middle-aged American men. All the subjects had high cholesterol levels when the research began, and they have been followed very closely throughout the ten years of the study.

In what must be the most important medical news of the decade, the Institute reported direct, overwhelming evidence that reducing cholesterol levels prevents heart attacks and the likelihood of heart attack deaths.

The study showed that for every 1 percent drop in cholesterol level, there is a 2 percent decrease in the risk of heart attack. When the cholesterol level was reduced 25 percent, the incidence of heart disease fell 50 percent. Over the ten years of the study, those who were on both low cholesterol diets and drugs had 24 percent fewer fatal heart attacks than those who did nothing to control cholesterol levels.

This evidence is impressive. It conclusively shows that lowering blood cholesterol levels is crucial for avoiding heart disease.

But how low should cholesterol be? *Much* lower than hitherto believed, according to *Science Digest,* which quotes Dr.

William Castelli, the present director of the famous Framingham Heart Study involving five thousand residents of a Boston suburb:

> Half the heart-attack victims in America have a cholesterol level between 150 and 250, but because their total cholesterol is under 250 (the acceptable limit of normal), they are being completely ignored by physicians. You see, if your cholesterol level is under 150, you are not going to have a heart attack— even if you smoke, have hypertension and all the other stuff.[1]

What this indicates is that although any reduction in cholesterol levels is helpful, to be completely safe from the ravages of coronary artery disease it is necessary to cut the cholesterol level *far below* the amounts currently considered "normal." And the catch is that the commonly accepted ways of lowering cholesterol are insufficient to lower cholesterol to a level that is really safe!

Diet and Exercise Are Not Enough!

The most commonly recommended way of controlling blood cholesterol is through diet. Much has been written about this over the past few decades. The recommendations of the National Health, Lung, and Blood Institute study are straightforward and familiar:

- cut down on saturated fats and high-cholesterol foods (lists of appropriate foods are widely available)
- substitute fish and poultry for high-cholesterol red meats whenever possible
- eat only two or three eggs a week
- limit shellfish and organ meats such as liver to small portions each month
- cook with low-cholesterol vegetable fats (such as corn oil, olive oil, or safflower oil—and margarine made from such oils) instead of saturated animal and vegetable fats (such as butter or coconut oil).

---

1. Quoted in *Science Digest*, April 1985, p. 35.

It is recommended that each person limit himself or herself to fewer than 300 milligrams of cholesterol per day. Since most of us consume more like 400–600 milligrams, the amount should probably be halved.

But there is a catch when it comes to controlling cholesterol through diet. The National Health, Lung, and Blood Institute study showed that change in diet was only able to bring about a *4 percent lowering* of the level of cholesterol in the individuals studied! (Other studies put the figure at 10 or 11 percent.) This means that if the blood cholesterol level is, say 250 milligrams per 100 millilitres (abbreviated simply as mg%), even a drastic change in diet would lower it about 10 mg%—to about 240 mg%. Not much of an improvement, especially in view of the recent evidence that cholesterol level should be far below the commonly accepted norm of 250 milligrams. Remember, only about 10 percent of our blood cholesterol comes from food, anyway; the majority is produced by the liver.

There are drugs available that lower cholesterol, and these can be very important for high-risk individuals. But even a combination of low-cholesterol diets and drugs would only lower the cholesterol level to about 200 mg%, which is still above the level of totally "safe" cholesterol.

Exercise is another frequently cited way of lowering the risk of heart attack. Actually, regular exercise that is appropriately tailored to the individual age and level of fitness is helpful for almost everything. Prayer life, self-esteem, and mood as well as physical health and cholesterol levels seem to benefit from regular physical exercise.

But do you recall that a very famous runner dropped dead of a heart attack few years ago? He had even written several books about the benefits of running. But his hours on the track were not enough to prevent fatal coronary artery disease. While heredity probably played a significant role in this man's heart disease, his is not an isolated case. Enough people drop dead on running tracks every year to show that exercise by itself is not enough to prevent heart attacks. Something more is needed.

Adrenalin Is the Other Part of the Picture

I believe that much of the current literature concerning cholesterol and heart disease fails to take into consideration the close connection between high cholesterol, stress, and adrenalin arousal. This, in my opinion, is the "missing link" often ignored when it comes to preventing heart disease.

An increase in circulating cholesterol during stress is part of the body's reaction to threatening stimuli. Coupled with this elevation, or perhaps resulting from it, is a corresponding elevation of adrenalin. The rise in cholesterol and adrenalin levels raises blood pressure and increases the circulation of blood to tissue that needs it.

The evidence that stress raises cholesterol levels is abundant. Accountants' cholesterol levels have been found to be highest at tax time; medical students register 10 percent higher during examination time; employees fired from their jobs show a 10 percent drop in cholesterol when they finally secure new work.[2]

Emotional upsets such as fear, anxiety, depression, and anger can be shown to raise both adrenalin and cholesterol levels. Depression especially has a marked effect, particularly on adrenalin, as does general emotional instability.

As far as personality characteristics are concerned, two personality "dimensions" have been found to be associated with elevated cholesterol:

- "overactivity" (excessive competition, aggression, and impatience)
- "overcontrol" (exaggerated sense of responsibility, conformism, and low self-esteem).

---

2. L. Van Doornen and K. Orlebeke, *Journal of Human Stress,* December 1982, pp. 25–26.

Both these personality traits are associated with the Type-A behavior pattern, which is known also to produce higher levels of adrenalin. Another psychological factor contributing to the recruitment of cholesterol appears to be that of "perceived helplessness." It appears from recent research that when a person is caught up in a situation about which he or she feels helpless and has no control over the outcome, cholesterol as well as adrenalin levels increase significantly. For the Type-A person, who already has high levels of these, the aggravation only makes the risks greater.

Controlling Cholesterol and Adrenalin

What does all this mean when it comes to preventing heart disease?

First of all, since blood cholesterol levels, adrenalin levels, and heart disease are closely linked, it is important to have the blood cholesterol tested regularly. And such a test should include determining the ratio of LDLs to HDLs, not just the combined total level. It is recommended that blood cholesterol be checked every five years or so after age twenty or twenty-one. Your physician will advise you as to what normal levels should be—but push for a "conservative" recommendation to be on the safe side.

Second, it is a good idea to maintain a blood cholesterol level that is well *below* what is usually considered the norm. This is done to a certain extent by diet, medication if necessary, and moderate exercise, but it also involves controlling adrenalin levels.

This brings us to the third point, the one crucial to this study: We must *also* educate ourselves in better stress management so as to reduce the damage that our stress hormones can cause in the presence of even moderately elevated cholesterol. In other words, adrenalin management cannot be separated from cholesterol control.

A recent survey by the same national institute that conducted the cholesterol study showed that only 39 percent of the physicians surveyed believed that lowering cholesterol would help prevent heart disease.[3] I don't think this low percentage is due to ignorance. It simply shows that other factors besides cholesterol play a part in heart disease—and a major factor is stress.

Lowering adrenalin in the blood, whether by relaxation or psychological means or by blocking the receptors of adrenalin through drugs, lowers blood pressure, and this lowers the risk of heart disease. And lowering the adrenalin level would also contribute to lowering the cholesterol level. So it is clear that adrenalin management and cholesterol management must remain closely tied. Both together are far more effective in preventing heart disease than either alone. In part 3 of this book we will look more closely at specific techniques of adrenalin management.

Before going on to other topics, I would like to add a warning when it comes to diet and exercise as means of controlling cholesterol: Remember that stress and cholesterol are closely related. And it is possible to become so intense and competitive in exercise or even diet that stress levels remain elevated instead of being depleted. Adrenalin can be recruited by challenge and excitement as well as trauma.

Instead of producing peace and relaxation, intense competition can make us frustrated and angry and recruit high levels of adrenalin—even in basically healthy activities. We can run ourselves into the ground every day and still not be protecting ourselves from heart disease if we maintain an aggressive, overcompetitive attitude. Constantly racing against others or even yourself ("I'll be even better at staying on my diet today"), can continually trigger a fight or flight reaction with its attendant high cholesterol!

There is only one way to diet or exercise in a healthy, stress-lowering way, and that is to avoid frustration, overcompetitiveness, and hostility while you're doing it. St. Paul summed it up well when he said, "and the peace of God,

---

3. *Science Digest,* April 1985, p. 35.

which passeth all understanding, shall keep your *hearts* and *minds* through Christ Jesus" (Phil. 4:7).

So, before you jog, cycle, do your push-ups or eat your fish, do one important thing: Make sure you are at peace with yourself, the world, and with God. It is my hope that the suggestions in this book will help you do just that.

8

Finding the
Source of Your Stress

There was a time when people knew what stressed them. Life was simple and decisions relatively easy: "Should I eat or should I sleep? Should I hunt or should I gather berries?"

Occasionally, however, the pursuit of a small animal through the jungle brought an ancient hunter face to face with stress in the form of a saber-toothed tiger! Instantly the hunter's stress response system went into action. Adrenalin surged in the hunter's body to get the muscles primed and the nerves steeled for action. Now the decision was: "Should I fight or should I run for my life?" The hunter's heart pounded and his breathing quickened as he looked intently at the eyes of his adversary.

Tense moments passed. But apparently the beast wasn't hungry. After a quick snarl, it turned slowly away and vanished into the shadows. The crisis was over. The stress was past. Only the hunter's hungry stomach growled its disappointment.

Modern Jungles

The days of confronting saber-toothed tigers are long gone, of course, but for many the modern jungle is just as dangerous. Perhaps it is even more so, because today's tigers are not as easily recognized and dealt with. They hide in crowded buses, sit next to us on overnight plane connections, and scream at us over noisy telephones. There are many new beasts that can set the heart racing and the ears pounding far more readily than four-legged, slinky, silent kings of the jungle.

Unfortunately, our body systems were designed for jungle hunts and not traffic jams, cats that occasionally confront us, then slink away and not neighbors who stay put. We are better at meeting challenges that can be dealt with physically rather than psychologically.

June knows today's jungle well. Each day she sees it down in the valley out of her bedroom window—a tall forest of concrete enveloped in a dingy cloud of smog. On the way into the jungle she must maneuver through junglelike tracks with a reckless driver both behind and in front of her. The roar of honking horns is deafening and her heart races. Her teeth hurt from being clenched, and no amount of underarm deodorant copes with the flood of perspiration. Her saber-toothed tiger wears a red-striped tie most days and growls instructions and grunts dissatisfactions. And he prefers postponing her vacation to scratching her arms with his claws.

What is the source of June's stress? It is everywhere and in everyone, it seems to her. Where can she place her finger and say, "This is my problem; this is where my stress originates"? She can't "run" because she doesn't know what direction is safe. She can't "fight" because she's not sure who the enemy really is. The modern jungle is too big, too complex, too confusing for her to make any sense out of it. So June sits behind her desk, stomach churning and back muscles knotting, and reaches for the berries of her jungle—two aspirin and some Maalox.

The Many Sources of Stress

There are many experts today who are concerned over the "stress epidemic" in our culture that seems to be creating a mass "fight-or-flight" reaction. Dr. Joel Elkes of the University of Louisville says, "Our mode of life itself, the way we live, is emerging as today's principal cause of illness." [1]

---

1. Quoted in *Time*, 6 June 1983, p. 48.

He is absolutely right. It is not just Exxon tigers or Izod alligators that are our stressors, but every turn of each normal day. This makes it very much more difficult to pinpoint the source of stress. It is camouflaged by subtle shadows of normality and stripes of respectability. And if we don't know what the source of our stress is, we will probably not be very effective in coping with or removing it.

Stressors That Easily Elude Recognition

There can be many sources of stress that elude recognition in the average person's life, and I will discuss some of these shortly so as to help you be a little clearer about where yours comes from. Before I do so, however, I want to emphasize again the importance of not looking for your stress *only* in the calamities of life. While major life changes such as divorce, death of a spouse, or losing a job certainly generate stress, the *greater* source of stress for most of us are those life issues that can be called "minor hassles." There is a growing body of evidence that the everyday minor annoyances of life contribute as much, if not more, to stress disease than major life traumas. They certainly are around a lot more! The panic of getting ready every morning may be as damaging as watching interest rates going up and constantly bickering with a teenage son more than getting fired. If we don't watch these day-to-day hassles they can eventually kill us.

How can we know if these everyday sources of stress are getting to us? I have devised a brief test that might help pinpoint them. Answer the questions on it as honestly as you can, then add up your "score" according to the directions. See Appendix 1 for how to interpret the results.

Uncommonly Recognized Stressors

The more we know about where our stress comes from, the easier it will be for us to deal with it. Hidden or unrecognized stress is the most damaging of all; it tends to create more fear than is appropriate for the danger.

FIGURE 5
Everyday Hassles Test

Answer each question "yes" or "no." Give yourself one point for each "no" answer on questions 1 to 5 and one point for each "yes" answer on questions 6 to 10.

QUESTION	YES or NO	SCORE
1. Are you friendly toward **all** of your neighbors and work colleagues?	NO	1
2. Do you, on a daily basis, enjoy your work?	YES	
3. Do you feel financially secure?	NO	1
4. Does life seem meaningful most of the time?	NO	1
5. Do you feel in control of your life?	NO	1
6. Must you combine housekeeping or parenting with having to earn a living?	YES	1
7. Are you a single parent?	NO	
8. Do you feel angry toward someone or irritated by something at least once a day?	YES	1
9. Do you often (more once a week) have sleepless nights?	NO	
10. Are you frequently in a hurry?	YES	1
	TOTAL	7

What are some hidden stressors—some less obvious sources of stress that we often overlook? In this section I want to examine three of the most common: people, pain, and sin. In part 3 of this book I will be suggesting some positive ways to handle the stress that comes from these sources.

PEOPLE

I would guess that 95 percent of all our stress originates with other people. The reason is obvious: We can't avoid people! It is people with whom we must live and to whom we must relate. Relatives, friends, colleagues, strangers, fellow church members, employees, bosses, tax collectors, the police—all can be sources of stress.

Why do people stress us? Mostly because we need them so much! We all have a need to be loved and accepted by others, and many of us will go to almost any length to achieve respect or avoid criticism. We fear rejection because we so desperately want to be thought of as having value. Our egos crave the respect of others.

At the same time, these people whom we need are inconsistent. They can be loving or generous, but they can also be inconsiderate, selfish, self-seeking, and self-satisfied. They don't always follow through on promises; they break commitments at the bat of an eye. We have learned by experience that few people can be trusted entirely, and some appear to have outright intent to harm us.

In short, people cause us stress because everyone else is just like us—human! And that can be a real source of stress.

How do people cause us stress? Chiefly by making us fearful and angry, by threatening our security or withholding the approval we crave. And the emotions of fear and anger (which in turn causes more fear) bring out self-protecting instincts. When we become angry or fearful, the message we send our bodies is "Danger!" And our bodies respond by releasing adrenalin. (In chapters 10 and 15 I hope to present some constructive ways to deal with stress produced by the "adrenalin emotions" anger and fear.)

To compound the problem of people and stress, a great many of us have not learned, either in school or by the experiences of our lives, how to cope with the inconsistencies and inadequacies of others. Many of us lack assertiveness and find it difficult to claim the basic rights which are ours as humans—simple rights such as the right to be heard, to be treated with respect, to be able to say what we feel, and to get what we pay for.

Others of us lack the courage to be ourselves, or we don't even know what "being ourselves" means. "Who am I? What am I?"—these questions lie buried beneath so much of our tension. "If I am myself," we fear, "no one will like me." So we try to become what we think others want us to be, and this can be particularly stressful.

PAIN

The stress that pain can produce is very often overlooked. Most people, unless they have experienced a period of severe pain (and I don't mean an everyday headache or cut finger) have no idea how much stress it can produce. And pain is even harder to bear when we're not sure why we've got to suffer with it in the first place.

I have been relatively free of pain most of my life. But just three weeks before writing this chapter I underwent surgery. Mine was not a life-threatening problem. And my surgeon assured me that I could have the surgery under the new "one day" arrangement, in which the patient checks in to the hospital early in the morning, has the surgery, and leaves in the afternoon.

The surgeon's words to me were, "You might as well go home and suffer there, because you will be in a lot of pain afterwards." Well, dear man that he is, he didn't tell me how painful "a lot of pain" is, and he forgot to tell me how long it would last. I have never appreciated an effective painkiller as much as I did the first week after my surgery. (Thank God for analgesics!)

During the first week after my surgery I carried out an experiment. I tested my urine for stress hormones. I measured my skin temperature and checked for other physical indicators of stress. The results confirmed what I already knew: Pain produces stress. And if the pain continues for a long period of time—as happens with certain chronic disorders such as arthritis—it will produce stress disease just as surely as a hurried lifestyle will.

Our knowledge of the neurophysiology and psychology of pain is presently undergoing a dramatic expansion. While we haven't solved the all-important question of the meaning of pain, this knowledge is helping us provide a little more relief for those who must bear more of it than they deserve. In chapter 10 I will provide a few suggestions for making pain less stressful.

SIN

Most of us don't think of sin in terms of stress. We tend to confine it to the realm of the spiritual and see it as only affecting our relationship to God. But this is a very limited view of sin's damage. Sin hurts our minds and bodies as well as our spirits.

God's laws are always reasonable and intended to protect us from self-destruction. It's true that it is not always easy to determine the specific implications of God's laws. Most of us have known well-meaning parents, ministers, or Christian friends who have done damage by trying to impose on others their own narrow interpretations of what God expects.

But while much harm can be produced by inculcating neurotic guilt over petty and irrelevant life issues, God's laws themselves are certainly not petty or obscure or designed to create neurosis! Just the opposite—they are intended to show us how to live healthy lives, to protect us from harm. We know they are real, although we still violate them from time to time. "Evil is *against* us," I heard an old African preacher say once, and this truth has always stuck in my mind. Its design is our total destruction, and we need to be reminded of this often.

Why does sin cause us stress?

- It violates our deep convictions and values.
- It alienates the Spirit of God within us.
- It provokes a sense of guilt that can elevate adrenalin.
- It leaves us feeling vulnerable and depressed over our failures.

All of these can cause a state of internal alarm that causes an emergency reaction in our bodies.

Fortunately, however, God's provision for sin is perfectly complete. He offers us—if we will accept it—all that we need to handle the stress that comes from sin. I will be discussing this at some length in chapter 15.

Analyzing Your Stressful World

Whether your stress is produced by pleasant or painful life events—or by people, pain, or sin—the source of your stress must be clearly identified before you can take the next step of effectively managing the adrenalin that is triggered by your stress.

To help you in your analysis, I have devised a simple system of record keeping. Examine Figure 6. For a period of one week observe your daily activities closely. Every time you feel bothered, worried, angry, excited or stirred up in any way, place a small check (√) next to the category listed. (You may have to make the mark very small for some of the items because they will happen often! There won't be enough space if you don't keep your writing tiny.)

Notice that there are four major categories: home, work, recreation/church, and general. There is extra space for you to add any other category or specific situation.

At the end of the week, total up the number of marks against each specific event and you will be able to see where

FIGURE 6
Analyzing Your Stressful Environment

Period: _____ to _____(one week at a time)
Check, as often as necessary, the appropriate experiences as they occur.
Add any experiences personal to yourself.

HOME:	Checks	Total
Angry at spouse		
Angry at children		
Sexual difficulty		
Financial problems		
Family conflict		
Too many demands		
Trouble with in-laws		
Illness in family		
Major loss		
Blaming or projecting		
Houseguests or lodgers		
Remodeling or construction		
Wedding, divorce, etc.		

RECREATION/CHURCH:	Checks	Total
Could not relax		
Loneliness		
Destructive habits		
Inadequate exercise		
No support		
Interpersonal conflict		
No responsibilities		
Too many responsibilities		
Physical training		
Spiritual "awakening"		
Stimulating relationships		

WORK:	Checks	Total
Angry at boss		
Angry at fellow workers		
Making mistakes		
Noise irritants		
Too much work to do		
Too little work to do		
Change in pay or hours		
Pressure of deadlines		
Poor time management		
Poor prioritizing		
Lack of assertiveness		
Challenging project		

GENERAL:	Checks	Total
Difficulty sleeping		
Angry at neighbors		
Criticized by another		
Problems with car		
Weather conditions		
Emotions cause problems		
Too much excitement		

the source of your stress really lies. You may be in for some surprises. I've kept a record like this many times, and each time I have been amazed at how a particular life event can cause stress over and over again, yet elude recognition.

When you have identified your major stressor or stressors, you can more intelligently begin to plan a strategy for coping with them. And that is what the last sections of this book are all about.

9

How to Monitor Your Adrenalin Arousal

As I have attempted to show, the hyperarousal and excessive flow of the stress hormones, especially adrenalin, is the essence of the stress response. The first step toward learning how to control the secretion of adrenalin and thus reduce stress disease is to be able to recognize *when* we are being stimulated to produce more adrenalin.

There are many situations in which adrenalin arousal is appropriate. But many of us utilize more adrenalin for a given task than is really necessary by "psyching" ourselves up to it. Knowing when to allow arousal and when to switch it off is essential for effective stress management. If we know we are producing high levels of adrenalin, we can then exercise our freedom to choose. We can decide either that we need the adrenalin and therefore can let it do its work or we can decide that we need to conserve our energy and therefore slow down the adrenalin response.

The choice is ours, but we can only make an intelligent decision if we know how to tell when our adrenalin is aroused. My purpose here is to teach you how you can monitor your adrenalin arousal so that you can be free to manage it to your best advantage.

The Effects of Adrenalin Arousal

To be able to monitor adrenalin arousal requires that we first understand the effects of adrenalin on the body. Let's review the sequence of events from the moment we perceive a threat or challenge to the point at which our insides are bathed in adrenalin.

In response to a stressor, chemical messages are sent by the brain through the pituitary gland and nervous system to the adrenal glands (refer again to figure 1 in chapter 3). The release of hormones such as adrenalin by the adrenal glands produces the following changes:

- increase in heart rate
- increase in blood pressure
- decrease in size of arteries and capillaries in hands and feet (peripheral vasoconstriction)
- increase in muscle tension.

There are many other changes, but they are not as easily measured as these four. And it is the relative ease of measuring these reactions that makes this possible for us to monitor our adrenalin arousal (and thus the level of our stress).

Of particular interest from this standpoint is the constriction of the blood vessels in hands and feet. This happens because blood is needed more in other parts of the body such as the heart and lungs, and so the arteries and capillaries decrease in size to reduce circulation. As a result, the temperature of the hands, particularly the fingers, drops. This is the commonly experienced "cold hands" reaction of fear, anxiety, or excitement.

Because the temperature of the hands is so easy to measure, with or without a thermometer, we will be concentrating on it as a primary way of measuring adrenalin arousal. But it is also possible, with a little training, to monitor heart rate, blood pressure, and muscle tension. While this is a little more cumbersome, it can be very helpful in getting a clearer picture of your body's stress response.

The Purpose of Adrenalin Monitoring

My purpose in asking you to become more aware of your adrenalin arousal is to:

- help you better understand how your body responds to stress

- alert you to particular stressful events in your life
- increase your awareness of your freedom to choose whether or not you want to be adrenally aroused
- establish a baseline from which you can tell whether you are becoming more generally stressed
- tell you whether you are beginning to be master over your stress

Why is it important to be able to measure levels of stress? Because stress is elusive. Those who are most stressed are also the ones who tend to deny that they are stressed. It isn't until they suffer severe pain from their overstress that they begin to take notice. And even then the tendency is still to deny the stress and ignore the pain—or remove the stress symptom by taking a drug such as a painkiller or antacid. The objective picture that adrenalin monitoring gives is much harder to ignore!

Effective monitoring requires establishing a habit of taking the various measurements I will describe. At first this will be done *hourly*. But don't panic at what sounds like a time-consuming chore. Adrenalin monitoring takes only a few minutes and quickly becomes almost second nature. Before long you will be monitoring your stress without giving it much thought. Once you have established an adequate "base" of comparison and have developed a clear sense of how your system responds to stress, you will be able to ease up on the frequent monitoring and need only take one or two measurements during the day. Of course, the higher the levels of stress you discover, the more frequently you will need to measure your stress responses. If your early measurements show you are not very stressed, then less frequent measurements are adequate.

There is one important condition for a successful self-taught stress management program: *Be honest with yourself.* It is not a sign of weakness to acknowledge that you are overstressed! In fact, the strongest among us are frequently the ones under the most pressure. But it takes courage and maturity to be willing to admit that you may have a problem with the way you respond to that pressure.

Methods of Monitoring Adrenalin Arousal

The following methods may all be helpful in getting a picture of how your body responds to stress. If you have any questions about any of them, be sure and ask your doctor.

MEASURING HEART RATE

Your heart rate can be measured in a number of simple ways no matter where you are—at work or play. You can use one of the fancy new electronic devices designed for joggers and exercise buffs. They are portable, accurate, and easy to use; you place your finger into a special sensor and then read your heart rate on the display. Wristwatches are even available that allow you to rest a finger on one corner of the dial and get a heart-rate reading.

But why use expensive instruments? It's not hard to measure your heart rate the old-fashioned way—with your finger. Simply place one or two fingers (not your thumb) on the artery at your wrist. (A little experimenting will help you find it. Or, if you prefer, you can find the pulse in your neck, just under your jaw. Just don't press too hard, or you might cut down on the blood flow to your brain!) Count the pulses while you observe the second-hand on a watch or clock. You need only count for fifteen seconds and then multiply by four. No one need know you're doing this, so you can do it in meetings, during supper, or in bed.

Take your pulse often and write your pulse rate down in a notebook, together with a description of where you are and what you are doing so you can observe how various situations affect you. It is very easy to tell when your adrenalin is aroused; your pulse rate will change. It may only go up a few beats—or it may jump up to a very fast rate. The degree of change is what counts.

You will notice that almost every time you take your pulse, it will vary. It changes constantly—sometimes increasing, sometimes slowing in response to the many signals your heart receives. Observe what makes it go faster and what slows it down. After a while you will get so used to the time interval between beats that you need merely place your finger on your pulse to instantly tell whether your heart is beating faster than normal.

But what is a normal pulse rate? That depends on many factors. Athletes have a slow rate; children and some elderly people have a faster one—and all are normal. If you are a typical, healthy person your resting heart rate will probably be between seventy and seventy-five beats per minute. Generally speaking, the slower the better, although it is best to check with your doctor if you have any questions about what your heart rate should be.

For the purposes of adrenalin monitoring, find out what your pulse rate is when you are totally relaxed (the best time is before you get out of bed in the morning). Once you have established this normal, nonaroused baseline, you will immediately know when you are experiencing an adrenalin surge. And then you can then choose whether to implement one of the "management" techniques I will describe in the next section.

BLOOD PRESSURE

While it is not practical to carry around a sphygmomanometer (the "cuff" that measures blood pressure), blood pressure is nevertheless a measurement that should be taken regularly. Measuring blood pressure is important because it not only shows us when we are immediately experiencing arousal; it also tells us when we are adapting upwards or downwards in response to our *general* arousal. In other words, blood pressure tells if the *cumulative* effects of stress are getting to us. If I have a bad day at the office or with my students, my heart rate will fluctuate up and down. By the end of the day my heart rate may be normal, but my blood pressure may be up—indicating that the stress of the day is still bothering me. It helps me to understand my *overall* response to the *total* stress I am experiencing.

But let me sound a warning. The mere act of measuring

our own blood pressure can, at first, push it up quite high. Most of us are anxious about being "measured," and blood pressure can be *very* responsive to the fear of finding out that something is wrong. So don't pay too much attention to the first few readings you take. Just practice the measuring procedure repeatedly until you feel less threatened.

Many effective and simple-to-use blood-pressure instruments are now available at low cost. If you can afford it, buy one. If you can't, leave it alone and rely on other measures of your stress. The best is the type that is "electronic" and doesn't use a stethoscope. When you pump up the "cuff," the instrument emits electronic "beeps" that can be counted. Some models even deflate the cuff automatically, so you can't botch the job too easily! Home-monitoring kits come with complete instructions so I won't repeat them here. Practice until you can do it quickly and accurately and keep careful records.

Again, in order to establish a "base" from which you can tell whether you are having a stress reaction or not, you must measure your blood pressure regularly and write down the readings, with date and time. Begin by measuring it first thing in the morning. This gives you a good "resting" level by which to judge the rest of the day. Measure it again shortly after dinner when you've done your chores or put the kids to bed, then once more when you are in bed. It helps to be lying or sitting in the same place and position each time so that you don't get differences due to postural factors.

What is a normal blood pressure? It depends on your age and physical condition. A reading of 120/80 is considered "normal" for most people. (The first figure is the "systolic," or heart contraction, pressure; the second is the "diastolic," or heart resting, pressure.) A reading of 140/90 is generally considered to be the upper end of normal, provided you are resting and not having an adrenalin surge.

Consult your physician if you are at all concerned about your blood pressure or if you want to know what your normal blood pressure should be. Elevated blood pressure is dangerous in the long run, so get professional help quickly if you think you need it. Treatment by diet and drugs is very effective in lowering blood pressure temporarily, but long-term treatment also must include a change in your way of coping with stress eventually. Why not start now?

SKIN TEMPERATURE

We now come to what may be the most fascinating—and certainly the easiest—measure of adrenalin arousal we currently have at our disposal.

Do you remember that some years ago a craze for "mood rings" swept through the country? These rings were supposed to tell the mood of the wearer by changing colors. If the ring was blue, you were supposedly in a good mood— happy and peaceful. If it was black, you were supposedly down, depressed, angry, and miserable. In between were green and yellow, meaning you were emotionally "in between" yourself.

Now, these rings actually had an element of truth behind them! They functioned on the principle that the temperature of your skin, especially the fingers, goes up or down depending on what sort of reaction you are having to a life event. Built into the face of the ring was a temperature-sensitive liquid crystal that changed colors depending on the temperature of your hand.

But there were two things wrong with these mood rings:
- They did not measure "mood" at all, but adrenalin arousal! In other words, they measured your stress response. Of course, there is often a connection between your mood and your stress level, and that's why the rings seemed to work.
- They were too exposed to the atmosphere, so very often they measured the temperature of the air rather than the skin. They certainly didn't work when it was very cold or hot!

The principle that the skin fluctuates in temperature in response to stress and arousal is now well established. As I have indicated, it is called "peripheral vasoconstriction."

What happens is this: in response to stress, nerve and hormonal signals (including adrenalin) are sent to the blood vessels in the hands, which then constrict and reduce the volume of blood present in the fingers. The skin, therefore, becomes colder as the flow of blood (which is warmer than the air) is restricted. Whereas the blood temperature is 98.6° F, the air in a normal room will be about 72° F. If the blood vessels are completely relaxed, the temperature of the skin can go up to almost the blood temperature, even in a colder room. A very relaxed person could, therefore, achieve a skin temperature of around 94° F or higher. But when the blood vessels constrict, the temperature drops and can go as low as room temperature if the reaction is severe.

This fluctuation of skin temperature goes on all the time. Relaxation makes it get warmer, and arousal makes it get colder. For the most part, we don't feel these variations, because the brain blocks them out.

During stress, when adrenalin is increased, the drop in temperature of the hand can be measured quite readily. In recent years, little round plastic dots have been developed that have liquid crystal imbedded in them. These little dots change color in response to the change in skin temperature, just like mood rings used to. By placing one of these dots (the back is coated with adhesive) on the hand in a nonintrusive position, we have a simple yet effective measure of moment-by-moment changes in our level of adrenalin arousal. Obviously, if we place our hands in cold water the dot will measure the temperature of the cold water. But if we remain in a stable room temperature the stress dot will provide a convenient and accurate estimate of our skin temperature. As we will see, this can be a life-saver!

A supply of "temperature dots" can be ordered from one of several suppliers; see Appendix 2 for instructions on ordering. If you are careful not to lose the dot and place it on a smooth plastic surface when you take it off so as not to destroy the adhesive on the back of it, it will last you a long time. They should not be gotten wet or left lying in direct sunlight.

To use a temperature dot, remove it from its paper backing and place it on the back of the left hand (right hand if you are left-handed) in the web of skin between thumb and forefinger (see figure 7).

Notice, as you do so, that it immediately changes color, assuming, of course, that you are not overstressed. If you are, it will probably remain black. The colors range from black to yellow to green to blue, starting at about 80° F and going up to above 90° F. With the temperature dot you can estimate your skin temperature to within one or two degrees Farenheit. This isn't sensitive enough for clinical relaxation training, where we use instruments to measure skin temperature to an accuracy of one-tenth of a degree, but it is sufficient for the purpose of monitoring adrenalin arousal in real-life situations. Almost any small thermometer held between the thumb and first finger, including the little alcohol thermometers you get on desk calendars, will serve the same purpose as the dots, but measuring skin temperature with a thermometer is slightly more time-consuming and inconvenient.

The chart in figure 7 shows how the colors of the dot correspond to skin temperature. *Remember: The warmer your hand, the lower your arousal.* What you want to achieve, therefore, is *warm hands.*

What is a normal hand temperature? Ideally, one should try to relax so as to achieve a temperature over 90° F, preferably 92 or 94° F. This can be done when you are in a normally air conditioned room of over 70° F. If the room is colder than this it may be difficult to warm up to this level.

During stress, some people only drop one or two degrees. Others can drop as much as twenty and have hand temperatures as low as room temperature. By monitoring your skin temperature over a period of time, you will develop an understanding of your own unique responsiveness.

There are some factors other than stress levels that can affect the color of the dots, and it is helpful to keep this in

FIGURE 7
Using Temperature Dots to Monitor Adrenalin Arousal

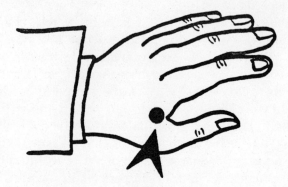

Place Temperature Dot Here

Color of Dot	Skin Temperature
Dark Blue/Violet	92 - 94° F
Blue	90 - 92° F
Blue/Green	88 - 90° F
Green	86 - 88° F
Green/Yellow	84 - 86° F
Yellow/Brown	82 - 84° F
Black	Below 82° F

mind to avoid false readings. Physical activity will lower the temperature and the color will change, just as will raising your hand above your head (which drains blood away). If the room temperature is below 65° F (air conditioning too high or wintertime), it will be very difficult for your body to keep the hands warm. The body conserves its heat by withdrawing the blood from the extremities, and this is *not* a stress response, just the body's normal adaptive response to cold.

Cold hands are also found in chronic migraine sufferers, certain diseases of metabolism such as diabetes, and in the elderly, where blood circulation is often diminished. "Raynaud's Syndrome," a disease of poor circulation, also causes cold hands. Excluding these factors, however, consistently cold hands should be taken as a sign of possible adrenalin overarousal.

Interestingly, both migraine headaches and Raynaud's Syndrome are now being treated by the use of biofeedback techniques that teach the patient to warm his or her hands. This is done by using equipment that gives the patient signals corresponding to the temperature of the hand (hence the term biofeedback, which means "biological feedback"). The patient then learns some techniques for achieving and maintaining warm hands by reducing adrenalin arousal, and the generalized relaxation that this creates helps increase blood circulation and prevents the migraines. I often use the same technique in my clinical practice for stress and find it very effective. Since such hand warming can only be accomplished by reducing adrenalin arousal, these biofeedback techniques can be very helpful for a wide variety of stress and related physical disorders.

Some people, notably those with Type-A behavior patterns and those who are prone to anxiety, have very "reactive" skin temperatures. In other words, their skin temperature changes often and shows large shifts up and down. Others tend to stay warm or cold all the time. By recording your temperature at hourly intervals throughout the day or during heavy or demanding work, you can get a clear picture of the stressful events that make up your day and how you respond to them. What you then do with this information is the subject of part 3 of this book. But first let me tell you one more way to get a rough idea of your skin temperature without any fancy gadgets.

I am sure you have shaken hands with someone and then been told, "My, your hands are cold!" This most often happens when you are under stress. Many ministers experience it after preaching and are sometimes embarrassed when shaking hands with parishioners. You can use this phenomenon to develop a simple test for adrenalin arousal. Since only the hands get cold under stress—not the face—you can place your hands on your cheeks and "take your temperature." If your hands feel colder than your cheeks, you are likely to be having an adrenalin surge. The greater the difference in temperature between hands and face, the greater the stress reaction. This method allows you to take your stress temperature at any time and in any place. You are then ready to implement the management techniques I will describe.

MUSCLE TENSION

It is not easy to measure this reaction without expensive equipment. In clinical biofeedback work we use an instrument called an "electromyograph" for this purpose. If you are seeing a psychotherapist who does biofeedback treatment, you can ask him or her to measure a few of your muscles and tell you how tense you are. If not, the best alternative is to develop some skill at subjectively assessing your own muscle tensions.

When you lie down at night, focus on each muscle group throughout your body and notice whether any of them feel tense. Do they feel "jumpy"? Is there pain anywhere? If there is, the feeling almost certainly means you are tense in the muscle where the pain is occurring.

Be alert for tightness in the stomach, discomfort in the

chest, twitching in parts of the body, a feeling of tightness in the jaw muscles, or sensations in the head above the eyes or toward the back. These can also be signs of muscle tension.

The relaxation techniques I will describe in chapter 11 can help you learn to lower your tension. Once you learn to recognize how it feels when your muscle tension is low, you can more easily tell when you begin to tense up.

Professional Ways of Measuring Adrenalin Arousal

In the event that you or someone close to you need professional help, I would like to briefly summarize how adrenalin arousal can be measured by a physician or stress psychologist.

The self-help techniques I have just described will only provide you with a rough (though still very helpful) guide as to the extent of your stress levels. To be more precise it is necessary for biofeedback instruments to be used and for the level of adrenalin and other critical hormones in either your blood or urine to be measured directly. Cholesterol level is also important and its assessment should be included in a thorough check-up of your susceptibility to overstress.

When measuring adrenalin, blood sampling is probably the first choice of the physician because the blood adrenalin level most closely reflects the ongoing state of your stress response at the time of collection. But there is a disadvantage to this form of measuring. Because blood sampling requires that a vein be punctured, many patients respond with an increase in anxiety during the procedure. This can easily elevate the level of adrenalin arousal and give a false positive stress reading. Blood levels of adrenalin do not, therefore, provide a foolproof way of measuring stress except in those cases where it is a chronic and persistent problem and the patient becomes accustomed to the procedure.

In the analysis of urine for adrenalin, fortunately, we have an easier solution. There is little or no anxiety associated with sampling urine, and there is usually an abundant supply available. The procedure itself does not produce stress.

To avoid momentary stress reactions from giving a false reading, however, the preferred method of urine sampling is to have the patient collect in a sterilized bottle the total production of urine over a twenty-four hour period, starting after the first voiding of the day. In this way, a sample of all the stress hormones secreted in the urine for a particular day's activities can be analyzed.

What is being measured in a urine analysis? The stress hormones produced by the outer layer of the adrenal glands, after circulating through the blood, are passed through the kidneys for recovery. A small percentage of the adrenalin and other hormones (especially cortisol) escapes the kidney's recovery system and passes into the urine. The amount passed by unstressed patients is very small. But during times of excitement or stress there is a great increase in the secretion of these hormones. The level of cortisol in the urine has thus become a popular choice for sensitively measuring the amount of physiological arousal a person is experiencing in response to stress.

If there is any question in your mind whether you need professional help in controlling your stress, I would urge you to contact your physician. He or she can guide you as to whether the procedures described above would be helpful and can refer you if necessary to a specialist in the fields of stress control and biofeedback.

Most people, however, can do a lot toward reducing their stress levels and healing their hurry sickness without seeking professional help. In the last section of this book I want to show some specific ways all of us can learn to manage the stress in our lives.

PART THREE

Healing
Your Hurry Sickness

"Another aspect of the phenomenon is our present
infatuation with speed. Having invented objects that can
travel, communicate, or fabricate other objects
at a greater and greater rate, we now seem willing
to subject ourselves to their demands.
Your great-grandfather, for example, trotting along
in his horse-drawn buggy at a leisurely pace, might very well
have stopped to chat with a passing neighbor
for ten minutes or so. Encased in your car, you will be
fortunate even to glimpse your neighbor as you each
hustle by. . . . Isn't there truth in the idea
that the faster a machine is made to operate,
the faster the operator feels *he* must think and act?"
—MEYER FRIEDMAN and
RAY ROSENMAN,
Type-A Behavior and Your Heart

"Don't copy the behavior and customs of this world,
but be a new and different person with a fresh newness
in all you do and think. Then you will learn
from your experience how his way will really satisfy you."
—ROMANS 12:2, LB

10

Managing Your Adrenalin

As I have already described, it is the excessive flow of adrenalin and related stress hormones that is the essential factor in stress disease. Your program of stress management will not be effective, therefore, unless you learn to bring your adrenalin production under control.

Can you so control your secretion of adrenalin that, rather than being the source of disease, it becomes your friend? Definitely yes. By following a few simple procedures you can live at peace with your body. It can be your servant rather than your master. All it takes is a little perseverance and some understanding of how and when you arouse your adrenalin.

If you know when you are adrenally aroused, then you can exercise your power of *choice.* You can choose whether or not you need the extra adrenalin, and then—if you don't need it—you can set about lowering it. One word of hope: It is *never* too late to start controlling the abuse of your body's defense system. Even if you are an "adrenalin addict" with advanced heart disease or you have already experienced a heart attack, you can prevent further damage and promote healing by learning to manage the behavior that creates the problem in the first place.

How Much Adrenalin Do We Need?

Dave is a pastor—a very competent and greatly loved pastor. He cares about people, and they respond by flocking to

his services and finding great joy in his ministry to them.
Dave is also an extraordinarily good preacher. He knows
how to communicate, and his deep voice resonates across
the pews as it proclaims truth and liberty in Christ.

But there is a problem in Dave's life. He is a little concerned
about how excited he becomes when he preaches. He "gives
it his all" as he totally surrenders himself to the task. But
afterwards he is totally exhausted, often feeling as if he could
not get up the strength to preach another sermon—ever. The
minutes after the last of his three Sunday services, when
he greets and chats with his congregation as they mill about
the church, are absolute misery for him. He feels drained
dry and wrung out with nothing to say and little incentive
to care. "What's wrong with me?" he asks. "Am I experiencing
some kind of spiritual depression?"

But Dave's is not just a spiritual problem. He has become
so accustomed to creating a "super high"—an adrenalin
surge—in order to accomplish the preaching task that he
is literally exhausting his body's defense system. The weekly
extreme ups and downs are beginning to take their toll on
his mind, body, and spirit. And he is developing a conditioned
fear of the period of "letdown" which always follows his
preaching. If he continues this way he may be forced to
leave the ministry. His extremely sensitive body will not be
able to withstand the abuse it is taking.

"I want you to let me teach you how to control your
adrenalin," I suggest to him. "You need to function at a lower
level of arousal at all times."

Dave is flabbergasted. While he doesn't understand the
physiology of his abuse, he believes that the only way he
can preach effectively is get "psyched up" to high levels of
adrenalin. He thinks he will be a failure if he doesn't. No
one will pay attention; people won't be gripped by the message; he'll just become like any other run-of-the-mill
preacher—these are his fears.

After explaining to him how his adrenalin system works,
however, I finally persuade him to *try* preaching with a lower

level of adrenalin arousal. I suggest the following program: Instead of spending hours each Saturday going over his sermon and "psyching" himself up, he is to relax and do something that will distract him from his sermon. Early Sunday morning, he is to skip the usual three cups of coffee he uses to get himself going, and after some prayer time he is to take a casual walk to the church, which is only about a mile away from his home. Rather than frantically reviewing sermon notes before the first service, he is to take ten minutes and do a deep muscle relaxation exercise.

Dave is apprehensive that next Sunday, but he faithfully follows my prescription. In the back of his mind he is afraid that he will flop horribly—but has the courage to try it anyway. To his surprise, he feels so much more peaceful through the whole time. His preaching, while not as physically energetic as before, deeply moves his congregation. And after the services he still feels energetic enough to enjoy moving among his people and feel authentic in his chatting with them.

Do you know what one member of his congregation says to him afterwards? "You were just as I imagined Jesus would be as a minister." His manner, rather than creating a feeling of frenzy, instilled a sense of peace, and people felt drawn to their Savior.

How much adrenalin do we need to perform God's work or, for that matter, any of the demands placed upon us? In most situations, not very much—and usually less than we think we need! Little of what we do is actually life-threatening or in the nature of an emergency, and we only hurt ourselves by reacting as if it were.

You may not have to preach each Sunday like Dave, and your life may be very routine or even boring, but you will have your equivalent periods of adrenalin demand:

- a deadline you must meet
- a neighbor who is antagonistic
- a child who is acting up
- a spouse who is seriously sick

- an elderly parent who needs to be cared for
- a program for some organization that needs to be planned
- a job that is not satisfying
- a lump that must be biopsied.

We all have our challenges and traumas that demand we go into an "emergency" mode of responding.

And how much adrenalin do we need to respond to these challenges? Again, *not as much as we think!* Stress can be aggravated by trying too hard. Most of us put forth too much effort for the task at hand. We overreact with fear to circumstances that are unusual. Why? I think most times it is because we lack faith. We overreact because we don't take God at his word; we don't trust our lives to his loving care—not completely, at any rate.

Our brains would work better if we didn't panic. Our actions would be more effective if we were not so tense; if we spoke our orders quietly and didn't shout them. Our hearts would certainly be healthier if we kept our adrenalin levels down as much as possible. And we can *choose* for ourselves how much adrenalin we need. It *is* possible to bring our propensity for high arousal under control.

Monitoring Adrenalin Arousal

I have devoted the whole of the previous chapter to showing you how to tell when your adrenalin level rises. When facing a particularly demanding or challenging situation, this is your first step: *Assess the level of your adrenalin arousal.*

Take this opportunity now to perform a self-monitoring exercise. Review your muscles for the telltale signs of tension. Are you clenching your jaw? What about your forehead or your neck; are the muscles knotted and strained? To improve your ability to sense muscle tension, try tightening these muscles slightly and notice how they feel. Now relax them again and notice the difference. Enjoy the freedom from tension.

Observe your hands; are they cold? They can turn blue before some of us pay attention! Test them against your face.

Do they feel icy? If so, chances are your body thinks it is in an emergency—assuming, of course you're not outside playing in the snow! (Only yesterday, I had to go and see my surgeon for a checkup following my recent surgery. Driving to his office I noticed my hands felt cold. I did the "face test" and they were freezing, so I settled back, consciously relaxed using some of the techniques I will explain in this section, and took a deliberate step of faith. Even if the surgery turns out not to have been successful, I decided, I would leave my condition in God's hands. A sense of peace came over me as I felt my adrenalin "switch off.")

Next, note your breathing. Does it seem shallow and fast? Can you hold your breath easily, or does trying to hold your breath make you feel panicky—as if you've just "got to" breathe. If you have these feelings, you are probably hyperventilating—a sign that your adrenalin is high.

Take your pulse. Is it slow and even? If it is faster than usual, and you are not physically exerting yourself, chances are you are on an adrenalin kick.

Make a Decision About Your Adrenalin Arousal

By monitoring your adrenalin arousal in these ways (especially after you have made a regular practice of noticing these signs), you can usually spot the early stages of an emergency response. When this happens, the next step is: *Ask yourself, "Do I need to be in a state of emergency right now, or do I need to accomplish some important task?"*

If the answer is *yes* (meaning you really *do* need the adrenalin), then go ahead and use all the adrenalin you can get going!

If your answer is *no*, then move quickly to relaxing your body, quieting your mind, and asking God to fill you with his peace. You don't need to be afraid. You certainly don't need an extra surge of adrenalin. Being calm and quiet will probably be more efficient for you at this point than being highly aroused.

Occasionally (and I mean *very* occasionally) you may not

be sufficiently aroused to cope with a demand. Perhaps because of fatigue, illness, or depression you just can't work up the energy you need to carry out your responsibilities. Then it may be appropriate—on a short-term basis only—to work at getting your adrenalin level up by doing something physical or by thinking through the implications of not taking action. This is one instance in which knowing how to "psych" yourself up may be useful. But if this problem is chronic, you should consult your physician, as there are some diseases that inhibit the activity of the adrenal glands and produce tiredness and lethargy.

How long should adrenalin be aroused? This is the all important question. Let us suppose you have been faced with a challenging life situation. On the way to an important meeting your car has broken down. "Emergency," you unconsciously shout to your brain, and adrenalin starts pumping. You move into quick action, find the nearest telephone, and decide who is the best person to call. You get someone to fetch you and take you to the meeting, leave instructions for the auto repair shop to tow the broken-down car, and arrange for someone to take you home afterwards.

All very efficient—and an appropriate use of adrenalin arousal. High adrenalin has helped sharpen your wits so that you can make decisions and take fast action. But then you get to your meeting and find that your heart is pounding, your hands are cold (everyone shaking hands with you remarks on it), and there is a slight tremble in your fingers. You're still on your adrenalin high. Is this necessary?

Obviously not. The emergency is past, but a vague fear keeps you on edge. Force of habit keeps your system in high gear, even though you're coasting downhill. This is the time to go into a relaxed state so as to quickly restore your system to normal.

Bring Down Your Adrenalin Level

Adrenalin surges should not be allowed to continue beyond the immediate legitimate emergency that provokes them. *As soon as possible* after the emergency, you should bring down your level of arousal. To let it continue at a high level or, for that matter, not even to be aware that you are still in an adrenalin emergency, is to court disaster in the form of stress damage. You need to move back to a nonemergency mode as quickly as possible.

I realize that this may sound easier than it really is to put into practice, and if you do not know how to relax your body and your mind it certainly will be difficult. The relaxation exercises I describe in chapter 12 need to be practiced ahead of time as a way of "innoculating" yourself by preparing for these emergencies long before you are confronted by them. The good athlete does not wait until the race before she prepares herself for the challenge and grueling physical demand. The airline pilot does not wait until an emergency before trying to cope with an engine problem. Weeks of practice—getting physically fit or rehearsing emergency procedures—precede the race or flying crisis. You cannot hope to be effective in adrenalin management unless you *first* master the techniques of lowering adrenalin during less pressured moments.

How Can Adrenalin Levels Be Lowered?

Once you have decided that you don't need the adrenalin you are recruiting (or once the emergency is over) it's important to bring the adrenalin level down as rapidly as possible.

If you can, it helps to excuse yourself and find somewhere to be by yourself for a few minutes. But if you can't, don't despair! You can just as effectively bring your adrenalin under control on a crowded train, in a busy shopping mall, at an intense board meeting, or during a final examination as you can in the quietness of your own bedroom.

Each of us will need to find the specific adrenalin-reducing tactics that work best for us. For many, this will be some form of "self-talk." Some people need merely say to themselves, "Now calm yourself. Life is not a hundred-yard dash. If you let down your adrenalin, you will be more effective and creative than if you stay panicked. God is still in control and a high level of adrenalin pushes him out. Be at peace." Others will need to be tougher on themselves. Find your own strategy of self-talk (some ideas are listed below) and tailor it to your personality. Be tough or tender—just convince yourself that you must get your adrenalin down.

The primary and most successful method for adrenalin reduction is *conscious physical relaxation.* When you relax the body, the mind *cannot* keep it in a state of emergency. A relaxed body begins to relax the mind.

Some exercises for learning to relax fully are described in chapter 12. Once you have learned them, you can go through them almost anywhere or anytime.

But you don't necessarily need formal exercises. If you are seated, get up and take a stretch. Walk around the table or down the corridor. Look through a window at the clouds outside. Go outside if you can; feel the sun and smell the flowers. Pick a leaf and note its intricacy and wonder. All the time, consciously relax your muscles. Those that hold the tension are rarely those that are needed to perform any physical task.

Remembering that the combination of self-talk and physical relaxation is usually effective in lowering adrenalin, try the following when you are in a situation where you want to lower the level of adrenalin in your system:

(1) *Remind yourself that you are just a very tiny cog in a very big machine.* If you stop playing Messiah, you will have considerably less stress!

(2) Remember that if you have been or are going to be successful, *it will probably not be solely because of your Type-A behavior.* Society does reward us for our hurriedness, but real happiness and long-term success come only from living a balanced life.

(3) If you feel you *must* succeed in the situation before you, then *ask yourself, "Is the price I am going to pay for this really worth the benefit?"* The answer will probably help restore a sense of balance and remind you of your long-term goals and values.

(4) Learn to *deliberately slow down.* Develop the ability to *choose* to go slow when you need to. What's the real hurry? The sun won't come up before tomorrow morning, no matter how much you rush. Few friends, fellow workers, or superiors will have any more respect for you because you "hurry" yourself. If anything, most would trust you more if you slowed down.

(5) *Quickly resolve those emotions that are adrenalin "biggies"*—such as anger, resentment, frustration, irritation, and excitement. Apologize if you are wrong. Bury your hurts that are due to oversensitivity and forgive those hurts that are due to others' insensitivity or cruelty. (See later in this chapter for some tips on how to do this.)

(6) *Review your life goals.* Ask, "Is the challenge before me absolutely necessary to my life goal?" I assume that God has a place in that goal. If so, then consider whether he would want you to be destroyed in your quest for success. Consider whether your goals need to change.

(7) *Look closely at the faces of those around you.* What do they tell you? Do they seem like friends or foes? Are you forgetting that they are people also, with rights, longings and aspirations, a need for love? Do them and yourself a favor by easing up your demands on them. When you do, a sense of peace will be restored.

(8) *Relax your expectations and enjoy the world around you.* Recover your *total* personality and poise. Try to be gracious and keep your perspective about what is really important and necessary.

It is hard to remain on an adrenalin high if you really believe what Jesus said is true: "So my counsel is: Don't worry about *things*—food, drink, and clothes. For you already have life and body—and they are far more important than what to eat and wear. Look at the birds! They don't worry about what to eat . . . For your heavenly Father feeds them" (Matt. 6:25–26, LB).

Why don't you, right at this moment, go and find a bird to watch? If you don't have any near your apartment or office, go to the park. "Look at the birds" is Jesus' prescription for hassled minds. I guarantee it will help you find peace. In fact, I am going to take a break right now and do just that! I think it will help me reduce the adrenalin I feel rising in my blood as I sit and write about it.

Planning Recovery Time

We cannot avoid all arousal all the time, nor should we even try. It is inevitable that there will be periods when our adrenalin is surging strongly and, rather than come down, it must stay up. When the task is important enough, we need all the energizing and enlivening we can muster!

Perhaps it's when a child is sick and needs constant attention over many days. Perhaps it's when we have planned a visit to our childhood haunts and find ourselves on a "temporary" high as we relive early life experiences. Perhaps it's when we have to complete a research project or host a special dinner party. Or perhaps it's when a friend or family member is in trouble with the law or has a terminal illness. Whatever it is, the task demands arousal, and there is no chance of it letting up until the task is accomplished.

What should you do in times like these? It is crucial that you plan adequate time for recovery. Sooner or later the crisis will be over, and that is when you must make time for adequate recuperation of your adrenalin system. This is simply a matter of responsible self-management.

I used to be the world's worst when it came to allowing adequate recovery time. As I mentioned in an earlier chapter, I am sometimes asked to speak at a retreat or deliver a series of lectures away from home. In the past, when this happened, I would leave my office around midday on a Friday, fly to the east coast, speak at a meeting that evening, present three seminars on Saturday, preach at two services on Sunday morning, and fly back to Los Angeles that afternoon, arriving home a little before midnight. And the next morning I would get up at six-thirty and be at my office for my first appointment at eight.

What's wrong with this? The reason ought to be clear by now! Such nonstop activity without adequate recovery time eventually takes its toll in terms of increased wear and tear on the body, accelerated cholesterol, and adrenalin exhaustion—not to mention possible heart disease.

No matter how I try to relax while I am away and engaging in such intensive activities, my system will stay aroused all the time. I sleep in a strange bed (which often reduces sleep effectiveness), meet new people (which creates certain anxieties), and fulfill a demanding speaking schedule (which keeps my adrenalin pumping all the time). When I come home, my body simply needs time out to recover and rebuild.

Fortunately, my eyes were opened a few years ago, and I saw what I was doing to myself. That is when I became determined to always build in recovery time. Now, whenever my schedule threatens to become especially demanding, I plan ahead for recovery time *afterwards*. For instance, if I have a long series of speaking engagements, I clear my schedule after that time for a period of rest. Sometimes it may only mean sleeping in a few extra hours the next morning and going to my office around noon. Sometimes it means I take a day or two to compensate for the lack of a "sabbath" rest. Sometimes it simply means that I schedule a day of "lighter" work. The specifics are not important, but the principle is!

Preparing for Times of Stress

Another way I plan ahead for times of extra stress is by scheduling to keep change during those times at a minimum. For instance, I keep my travel times as short as possible and seldom plan two speaking engagements to follow one after the other. Often we fail to realize just how arousing change is. Just being away from home, staying in strange places, and meeting new people can be enough to cause overstress. So in times of extra stress it helps to keep other change at a minimum.

Still other ways I prepare for a demanding schedule are:
- sleeping a little extra ahead of time
- cutting back on extraneous activities
- making sure I do my relaxation exercises faithfully
- planning all my time as efficiently as I can
- restricting the demands others impose on me.

This last takes a lot of assertiveness but is very important, especially in times of extra stress. We have to be *firm* with those who would clutter up our lives with trivia. We must be *clear* about our own priorities. And we must be *free* of excessive guilt about not doing what everyone wants us to do. As we get older (and I mean past thirty) we must become more determined to control our adrenalin arousal by managing the circumstances that create it as well as facilitating the conditions for its recovery.

Avoid the Adrenalin Emotions

Emotions have many different purposes in our lives. Some, for example, are designed to provide healing. Surprisingly, depression is one of these healing emotions. It serves to remove us temporarily from involvement in our environment so that our bodies and minds can be restored. (See my book, *Coping with Depression in the Ministry and Other Healing Professions.* Word Books, 1984).

Other emotions are "signals." They tell us something is happening to us—especially when something is wrong. Anxiety and guilt fall in this category. So also do those emotions that I call the "adrenalin emotions" because they tend to stimulate adrenalin production:
- anger
- frustration
- irritation
- resentment
- hostility.

These emotions can kill us prematurely. Most of us know other people who are destroying themselves by indulging in them excessively. These people get angry whenever they are disappointed. They become frustrated whenever they can't get their way. They hold grudges and carry resentment, fed by impeccable memories, whenever they are hurt. And unfortunately our culture glorifies these emotions!

Actually, the last three of the "adrenalin emotions" are very closely related to the first one—anger. And, simply speaking, *anger is bad for us!* Why? Because it triggers the "fight or flight" reaction more easily than any other emotion and can keep it going longer.

In its early stages, anger is simply a signal that we have been hurt or our rights infringed—physically or psychologically. The feeling of anger is the "pain" of our psychological makeup. It tells us that we have been violated. And at this point there's nothing wrong with anger.

But then, two things can go wrong:

• We don't pay attention to the anger.
• The anger feeling becomes translated into *behavior* such as aggression and hostility.

The ultimate purpose of anger is to prepare us to fight (it is the "fight" part of the fight-or-flight response). Anger creates in us a powerful need to "hurt back." Therein lies its greatest danger both to ourselves and others. But I am really not concerned about the effect of anger on others at this point; that is easy enough to figure out. What I want to emphasize is how destructive anger can be to *the one who is angry.*

Being angry for any length of time almost certainly increases the level of adrenalin, raises blood pressure, and causes skin temperature to drop. And the reason is simple: The body, fed by ideas from the mind, is kept in a constant state of readiness to fight. This heightened and persistent level of chronic hostility, like any form of continual overstress, will cause accelerated deterioration of the cardiovascular system and a host of other stress symptoms such as headaches, ulcers, and stomach problems.

Anger, with its cohorts of resentment, hostility, frustration, and irritability, will also be loaded with fear. We are afraid of those who hurt us, and the more afraid we are, the more we will tend to harbor grudges and keep our resentment alive. For legal as well as moral reasons, we can never repay those who hurt us, so we are left to suffer the consequence of our anger within ourselves. Those who hurt us then cause us double damage—the original hurt, compounded by the damage our anger will finally do to us.

This came home to me forcibly last September when I was on a speaking tour in Australia and decided I would learn how to throw a boomerang. Early one sunny morning during a break I enrolled in "boomerang school" at a nearby park. The instructor showed me how to stand, hold the boomerang, and throw it. I did. That little piece of twisted wood left my hand like a bullet, twirling furiously as it described a wide circle. Then, as I stood staring, surprised, it came back towards me. My instructor shouted, "Duck!" Luckily I did, or I would have been seriously injured. Boomerangs are dangerous! But so is anger. It injures the one who throws it about.

I believe very strongly that, while we must heed our feelings of anger just as readily as we heed a pain in the knee or tooth, we must learn to dispose of our anger as rapidly as possible. Paul's advice is absolutely accurate from an adrenalin-management standpoint: "Let not the sun go down upon your wrath" (Eph. 4:26). *"Get rid of all your anger very quickly"* was what he was really saying. Modern stress psychologists would say a loud "amen" to this, because bringing anger under control helps restore our adrenalin to its lower level once again.

In chapter 15 I will be talking about some spiritual antidotes to anger—and I believe that the only solution to deeply held anger is a spiritual one. But the following ways may help bring down the level of everyday anger in your life:

(1) *Make sure you include nonangry people among your closest friends.* Angry people fuel each other. If you are easily influenced by them, avoid them. Chronically hostile people

don't make good friends; their anger is too contagious.

(2) *Accept the flaws in your own personality.* If you are unduly sensitive to criticism, learn how to respond more constructively. If you keep expecting others to be perfect (because you fear your own imperfections), consciously give them the gift of "imperfection." Work at accepting them as they are, not as they measure up to some ideal.

(3) *Stop believing that anger is good for you.* It isn't. The feeling of anger is healthy *only* to the point that it alerts you to a violation of your rights. Thereafter, it is important to use constructive and not destructive means for coping with the hurt.

(4) *Be more assertive with people who hurt you.* Tell them they are violating your rights *before* you get angry. If they won't listen, avoid them. God calls us to love each other, but doesn't say we must place ourselves in the place of constantly being offended or punished. It's easier and more constructive to love some people from a distance!

(5) *Try to stop being critical of others.* Remember that the most common reason we find other people obnoxious is that they reflect our own weaknesses. Angry people see anger in others because they subconsciously recognize their own personalities. So work at seeing the good in others—perhaps you'll begin to become a little more like them.

(6) If there are life circumstances that are causing you ongoing hostility, *pray for God's wisdom* on what you should do. Perhaps you need the courage to move out or change your circumstances. Life is too short and too precious to be wasted on trying to make a good thing out of impossible circumstances.

How to Cope with the Stress of Pain

In chapter 8 I showed that pain can be an unrecognized source of stress. When we are in pain, our bodies react as to danger, and adrenalin levels go up.

Like anger, pain has a legitimate function; it alerts us to

something that has gone wrong. But after that initial purpose has been served, it can simply linger on as a source of stress. For people suffering from certain disorders such as arthritis, skèletal misalignments, and cancer, pain can be a constant and stressful part of life. To help cut down on the stress pain causes, the following suggestions may be helpful:

(1) *Try not to dwell on it.* Pain, like our other sensations, is affected by how much attention we focus on it. Athletes who are hurt while playing have been known to be unaware of their pain until afterwards. Partly this is due to high adrenalin, but it also occurs because the athletes get caught up with a distracting activity. When we are immersed in an activity or are diverted by interesting conversation or hobbies, pain is easier to tolerate. So if you are experiencing long-term pain, try to avoid boredom, inactivity, or brooding. This will *not* make the pain go away, but it might cut down on the stress pain causes.

(2) *Try to avoid becoming anxious.* Anxiety makes pain worse. I prove this every time I go to the dentist. If I don't worry, I feel less pain. If I fidget, become tense, and exaggerate my impending doom, I ache more—every prick of the needle hurts.

Try following the advice of Paul in Phillipians 4:6–7: "Don't worry about anything; instead, pray about everything; tell God your needs and don't forget to thank him for his answers. If you do this you will experience God's peace, which is far more wonderful than the human mind can understand" (LB). This isn't always easy, but with God's help it can really reduce the level of your stress.

(3) *Experience relaxation in between your periods of busyness.* I discuss relaxation in more detail in chapter 12; at this point I merely want to give a brief rationale for relaxation and show how it can reduce the stress damage pain does.

We have within our bodies a very effective pain-inhibition system. It is biochemical in that the body has its own powerful painkillers, the endorphins I described in an earlier chapter.

Certain natural experiences help to increase endorphins. For example, in the last stage of pregnancy the amount of painkiller in the mother's brain rises quite markedly in order to help relieve the pain of childbirth. And while during certain types of stress the high level of adrenalin arousal helps mask pain, *prolonged* stress ultimately depletes our pain protection systems.

Relaxation, however, creates a state of low arousal in which the body produces more endorphins. The more we relax, the more we protect ourselves from pain. So learning how to achieve deep relaxation and practicing often can dramatically reduce the amount of stress that comes from being in pain.

Medication for Overreactive Adrenalin Systems

There are those whose adrenalin systems are overly reactive. The slightest demand raises their adrenalin excessively. The system becomes very sensitive and overly active, the blood pressure soars, the heartbeat becomes erratic, and a feeling of panic sets in very easily. Sometimes this sensitivity is brought on by prolonged stress. Sometimes it is due to genetic factors or even disease.

Fortunately, effective medical treatment is available for this condition. Medication is available that can control our adrenalin production very effectively. While I do not advocate the excessive use of these drugs because they can tend to make our bodies "lazy," there are cases when they are appropriate. When there is a tendency towards severe panic attacks, high blood pressure, or erratic heartbeats, medication for adrenalin control may be needed. (A physician must prescribe it.) But *then,* as quickly as possible, the person being treated must *also* get help in managing stress through other means. The overreactive adrenalin system is merely a symptom that stress is out of control. Temporary help from medication should be followed by permanent help in rearranging values, habits, behaviors, and beliefs.

The medication used in treating severe stress or panic disorders is a combination of a "Beta-Blocker" (called this because it blocks the receptors that feed signals back to the adrenal glands) and a minor tranquilizer. A physician will know how to treat the condition or will refer the patient to someone who does know. The treatment is very effective, so it's important not to delay in getting this kind of help if it is called for.

One word of warning though—too much blocking of the adrenalin system can cause a special form of depression. It is similar to the "post-adrenalin depression" we experience whenever we come off a mountaintop experience. It is no cause for alarm, and it passes away fairly quickly as the body is restored to wholeness again.

11

The Secret of Sleep

Tonight millions and millions of Americans will crawl into bed, draw up the covers, snuggle onto soft pillows, and then try to go to sleep—without much success. They will toss and turn for a long time before finally slumbering off to dreamland. One estimate is that as many as *fifty million* Americans sleep poorly, if at all. For most of them, their sleeplessness will be caused by hyperarousal—they will be "high" on too much adrenalin.

Not only will they sleep poorly, but many will rationalize their sleeplessness by believing that they sleep too much anyway. I wonder who started this erroneous idea? More suffering and discomfort is caused by this faulty idea than I care to enumerate. The truth is that *we need all the sleep we can get* if we are going to survive stress disease. Sleep is an important antidote for the stress of everyday living, and those who sleep better are less damaged by their stress. I would even go so far as to say too much sleep is almost never a problem for normal people. Sounds revolutionary, doesn't it? But these are very considered convictions—so read on!

It is true that some people may use excessive sleep as a form of escape. When they are depressed or worried they stay under the covers and avoid life. But this is a symptom of some other disturbance and possible unhealthy way of coping with life. It is not what I am discussing here.

There are also some rare illnesses in which the brain keeps wanting to go to sleep. One of them is called "narcolepsy," a disorder in which a sudden urge to sleep overtakes the sufferer, usually during emotional excitement. All your muscles become paralyzed and you cannot resist the immediate onset of sleep. Another is "sleeping sickness," a disease caused by a bite from an infected tsetse fly which is usually found in Africa or South America.

But again, these are diseases—not normal states. For most of us, sleep is an important restorative and relaxing state of the mind and body, and we need as much of it as we can possibly get. We neither abuse it nor do we use it for unhealthy reasons. Despite this, we've been deluded into thinking we sleep too much, and I believe this is a significant factor in predisposing our culture to high risk for stress disease.

Some Disastrous Misinformation

One source for the idea that we sleep too much probably comes from research carried out in the early fifties. Some insurance companies wanted to know what the effect of sleep on longevity was, so they surveyed hospital patients and discovered that the longer someone slept, the shorter was his or her life expectancy. For many years afterwards, the popular belief was that if you slept too much you shortened your life. I remember reading about this in my early adulthood and deliberately trying to shorten my sleep time.

But what eventually came to light was that the hospital study was bad research! The investigators didn't reckon on the fact that hospitals tend to have a large number of terminally ill people anyway. And it is certainly true that when you are very sick you sleep a lot more. Their statistics were slanted by erroneous assumptions made from observations of sleeping patterns at the end of life.

This research has long since been debunked, yet many still believe that you'll live a shorter life if you sleep longer or you'll live longer if you sleep less. False! Generally, women sleep more than men yet they live longer! The truth of the matter is that Americans in general do *not* get enough sleep. Most adults are chronically tired or sleepy in the daytime because they don't get to bed at a reasonable hour. This means that they're not alert enough during the day; they lack the ability to think creatively; and their work efficiency is reduced. Most important of all, their adrenalin level is too high and altogether this makes for a bad stress-producing package. Effective stress management requires that we learn how to sleep better and longer, and my purpose here is to help you improve your sleeping habits so as to improve your resistence to stress.

It is true that sleep needs do vary among individuals and at different stages of life. These variations are, in my opinion, not as great as we have been led to believe and reflect variations in habit and levels of arousal as much as they do biological rhythms. Some people condition themselves to behave as "night" people, while others consistently reinforce fewer sleeping hours. But again, these variations seem to be more psychological than physiological.

What Causes Sleeplessness?

There are many reasons why a person doesn't get a good night's sleep. These include poor sleeping habits such as going to bed too late or at irregular hours, unfamiliar surroundings, too much anxiety, debilitating depression, or the abuse of drugs and alcohol.

However, one very simple, commonly overlooked factor contributing to sleeplessness is elevated adrenalin. If you are excited, charged, energized, or challenged, your adrenalin goes up—and you feel less need for sleep. Your adrenalin can also be triggered by worry and anxiety, and these will also keep you awake. The rule is simple: *Whenever adrenalin goes up, your sleep needs come down!*

It is here we can see a connection between the incidence of heart disease and poor sleeping habits. I am currently conducting a research project that is looking at the sleeping habits of heart-disease victims. I believe that excessive adrenalin production is the major cause of heart disease, and since elevated adrenalin also inhibits sleep, I feel there must be a connection between premature heart disease and a reduced need for sleep. If we can establish that those who sleep poorly or insufficiently are at greatest risk for heart disease, we can have a powerful diagnostic pointer for cardiovascular disease. More importantly, it is just possible that getting someone to sleep longer will help to bring down adrenalin and prevent heart disease.

It is not clear which comes first in this chicken or egg issue. Is it the lowered adrenalin that increases sleep and protects the heart, or is it the extra sleep that lowers the adrenalin? Actually, it doesn't really matter which comes first—as long as we achieve the desired end result.

The limited number of heart disease sufferers I have studied so far have all confirmed my suspicion; they almost all have bad sleeping habits. They don't sleep enough; they sleep very lightly; they can't get to sleep easily; or, if they do sleep, they wake up early and then can't get back to sleep again.

Why? Their minds are very active and they are too excited or fearful most of the time. Their minds won't give the adrenalin system any rest. Instead of sleeping, they use the nighttime to finish projects, think up new challenges, or worry about their fears. Not surprisingly, many then find it quite easy to sleep during the daytime.

How Much Sleep Do We Need?

This is the million-dollar question, and I know I am going to ruffle quite a few feathers with my answer! If you believe you only need five hours sleep, chances are you'll only sleep five hours. Our behavior tends to be consistent with our beliefs—that's a psychological fact! To sleep longer, you need to be convinced that you need more sleep—so let me try some persuasive reasoning.

There is no absolute and definitive answer to the question

of how much sleep we *really* need (as opposed to how much we *think* we need). When our adrenalin is elevated our felt need for sleep diminishes. I know this because every time I am faced with an unpleasant or novel demand on a certain day, I tend to wake up (or rather be woken up by my adrenalin) earlier than usual and do not sleep as much the night before. It's as if my body knows that I have an extra demand or challenge facing me and it provides me with extra energy in preparation for it, but at the expense of my sleep. This is no problem if it only occurs infrequently. Whenever I have a period of extra work or am facing deadlines that must be met, my need for sleep diminishes. My mind tells my sleep control center that I can cope with less "lullaby." *But*—and this is the rub—I pay for my lack of sleep later! As long as my adrenalin is up, I'm fine and don't feel the need for the sleep. My adrenalin keeps me awake by providing extra energy, but it is also reducing my reserves. When it finally lets up and I "crash," I will be more fatigued than usual, even depressed from the exhaustion, and will require extra sleep to compensate for the overuse. The reduced need for sleep produced by my elevated adrenalin is not a healthy state.

How can so many people sleep so few hours? I believe it is because they are operating on too much adrenalin. (I am not talking at this point about the reduced need for sleep of the elderly, which may be the result of reduced blood flow in the brain.) People who sleep little have functioned this way so long that it has become a way of life for them. Their systems are highly aroused and they seldom relax enough to achieve lengthy sleep.

Whether or not this is destructive in the long run we don't yet know. Perhaps some people manage to achieve an optional balance between wakefulness and sleep and thrive on this. But I suspect there are only a very few in this category; most people who operate on very little sleep are probably suffering from bad early training and mistaken beliefs about sleep. For many, unfortunately, that isn't the end of the story. They will pay for their lack of sleep at some later time in terms of increased wear and tear on their bodies.

This is where I believe those sleep researchers who have tried to determine what our normal sleep needs are have missed the mark. In trying to find out how much sleep we really need, they have surveyed large numbers of urban adults, asking, "How many hours do you sleep?" What they have found is that the average amount of sleep that a normal person says he or she needs is between five and seven hours a night, with most around six or seven hours. This type of survey research is misleading, in my opinion, because the majority of the persons we encounter in our urban society are Type As—highly driven, highly stressed, and performance-oriented. They suffer from too much adrenalin arousal as a matter of course, so how can their sleeping habits be labeled as "normal"? If most of us are not sleeping enough as it is, we are not the ones to ask what "normal" should be!

What we need is research that will look at healthy, low-stressed people and determine how much sleep *they* need. This should then become the norm. My prediction, based on years of clinical experience, is that it will be a lot higher than the five to seven hours typically reported, and more like eight or nine hours per night. Who knows, it might even be ten!

It is my belief that for good stress-disease prevention, the average adult needs between eight and ten hours of sleep each night, with some going as high as eleven hours. There are some individual differences (such as age, lifestyle, and physical health) that will vary the actual amount needed, but an average of nine hours seems to offer the best protection, according to my clinical experience. Under conditions of high stress, the apparent need for sleep may diminish and extra sleep should be provided as soon as the stress period is over. If the stress demand continues, then extra "rest" time should be provided even if sleep is not possible. I am convinced that most of us could improve our physical and emotional health dramatically if we just slept or rested a little longer than we usually do in our highly driven culture.

"Ordinary" Insomniacs

One adult in four has insomnia, according to the sleep research center at Stanford University. They have trouble either falling asleep or staying asleep. They approach bedtime with a high state of dread and pray for the night to pass quickly. Some experience this only occasionally, while for others it is a chronic problem. The chronic sufferers depend almost entirely on sleeping pills for what little rest they get.

My purpose here, however, is not to focus on the problem of persistent insomnia (which calls for professional help) but on the more common problem of insufficient sleep, either self-induced or without choice.

We all experience temporary bouts with insomnia. It happens in the healthiest of people but mostly it comes on when we are overstressed. Seldom does it happen when we are on vacation—unless our idea of vacation is mountain climbing in Tibet.

Many people don't believe they should sleep very much, so they wake themselves up with alarm clocks or deliberately stay up late at night working or watching TV. They may label themselves as "night people"—except they get up early, too. (Other "night people" prefer to work late and then sleep into the day. They may or may not be getting enough sleep. And I think many of those who think they *do* sleep enough may be deluding themselves.)

Most of those who sleep very little *enjoy* their reduced need for sleep, believing they are more efficient and productive because they don't sleep as much. In many cases, this is simply not true. But even if they are right, there is possibly a price many of them pay for this "efficiency." It is the same price you pay for using a small motor to do a big motor's job—*burnout*. The body is like a motor that can become overheated and overused if it doesn't have enough rest time. And while it may seem to be working efficiently, it is wearing out before it should.

What Happens When We Sleep?

Sleep, "tired nature's sweet restorer," is still a mystery. Despite years of research, no one really knows what happens when we sleep or even why it is necessary for us to sleep at all, except that sleep plays some significant role in restoring damaged cells and replenishing depleted energy.

Research on prolonged sleep deprivation—during which people are kept awake for many days—hasn't helped solve the mystery much either. In fact, it has been quite misleading, because you cannot equate artificially induced sleep deprivation with the reduced need for sleep due to adrenalin arousal. The one is from without, the other from within— and this makes all the difference in the effect it has on the body.

What happens when we go to sleep? After about fifteen to thirty minutes of relaxation, the prospective sleeper reaches a stage of semiconsciousness which is neither waking nor sleeping. Most think they're still awake because they can think and hear noises, but they are nevertheless in a state of early sleep. After a few more minutes they suddenly fall into unconsciousness. That final shift from drowsiness to sleep only takes a second or two, and none of us are around to see how it happens in ourselves. As we go from a state of semi-awareness to deep sleep, the brain's electrical waves get slower and slower until finally, after about ninety minutes, dreaming becomes possible. Then our bodies jerk mildly and our eyelids flutter.

The transformations that sleep brings to the body are quite obvious. We breathe more slowly, our eyeballs turn up and out, our fingers grow cold and our toes warm. Blood pressure falls rapidly and is lowest about three hours after the onset of sleep. We change positions from twenty to sixty times during the night without knowing it, and for a few moments every ninety minutes or so we may return to semiconsciousness for a brief while. Then slowly (unless something like an alarm clock disturbs the process) our sleep becomes lighter. Consciousness flickers, fails again, flickers . . . and then we are awake.

Perhaps we'll yawn to inhale extra oxygen and lower the carbon dioxide accumulated in the body as a result of muscular inactivity. We might still feel tired, especially if our adrenalin is low, but this isn't necessarily a bad sign. To wake up tired, if we have slept long, can be a sign that adrenalin arousal has been reduced to a low level, and this is good news if we are fighting stress disease. After three or four nights of deep, long sleep, the feeling of tiredness on waking passes off, and we wake up refreshed and replenished in body and spirit.

Types of Sleep

There are basically two types of sleep: dream sleep and nondream sleep. They are also known as "REM sleep" and "NREM sleep." The acronym "REM" simply stands for "rapid eye movement," because it has been found that during dream sleep the eyelids make rapid jerking movements while the eyeballs move around. "NREM" simply means "non-REM" or nondreaming sleep.

What functions do REM and NREM sleep serve? NREM, or nondreaming sleep is a lighter stage that seems to be important for biochemical restoration of the brain. REM or dreaming sleep is the deepest stage and is important for the consolidation of memory and learning, as well as for sorting and storing information in the brain. We need about 25 percent of our sleep to be of the REM, or dreaming, type and the remainder to be NREM. The lighter NREM sleep is important to REM sleep, because it is only after a certain amount of NREM sleep that we can pass into REM sleep. Without NREM sleep, dreaming can't occur.

When we first go to sleep we are in nondream sleep. Then, about every ninety minutes or so, we pass into dream sleep and can stay there for a few or many minutes. After dreaming for a while (and we may or may not remember our dreams), we may return to very light sleep or even wakefulness.

Since light, NREM sleep is so important, and since we can often think we are awake when we are in fact semiconscious, it is important not to force ourselves into full wakefulness during these periods of nondreaming sleep. Many people will get out of bed, go to the bathroom, eat a snack, or watch TV—thinking they can't sleep—when they were actually in a light sleep! But getting up usually brings them to a state of real wakefulness. If instead they would just lie still and relax, realizing they were experiencing an important part of the sleep cycle, they would soon go back into a deep sleep again.

This dipping in and out of deep sleep is normal—in fact, there is no other way to sleep. We only create sleeping problems for ourselves if we fail to understand the value of light sleep and semiwakefulness. If, out of frustration, we force ourselves to true wakefulness during these times, sleep will almost certainly be gone for the rest of the night. Our adrenalin arousal will see to that!

Determining How Much Sleep You Need

Whether you are a "night" person or not, and whether you think you sleep too little or too much, the first step towards developing a healthy sleep habit is to determine how much sleep *you* need. Forget about everyone else—you might just be a little different!

There are two ways you can determine how much sleep you need. The first way is to begin by adding sleep in half-hour increments to your existing sleep period by going to bed earlier or waking up later. But give yourself time to adjust to each change. Add the first half-hour, then keep the new schedule for five to seven days. Observe what happens to your emotions, creative thinking, and energy level.

The reason you must let the extra sleep "settle down" for a few days is that if you are trying to lower your adrenalin at the same time, you may initially feel *more* tired upon waking. This, as I have already explained, is a *good* sign. Welcome it! By the fifth or sixth day, the benefits of the extra sleep will be obvious to you. Then add another half-hour of sleep and again keep this schedule for five to seven days so as to observe the results.

Sooner or later you will get to the point of no further improvement, and it will be easy to decide how much sleep makes you feel alive and function at your best. For most of us it can be between one and two hours *more* than we presently sleep.

The *second* way to find your optimal sleep period is to recall your last extended vacation and try to remember how much sleep you got during the second week of that vacation. If it was a *real* vacation it probably went like my last one in Hawaii. As I related earlier, for the first four or five days I was restless. I kept waking up early but still feeling tired. I fidgeted, couldn't sit still for long, and kept wanting to "do something." I was experiencing "adrenalin withdrawal" because my body wasn't used to the reduced demands of vacation life.

But slowly I settled down and my sleep improved. By the end of the week I could get to sleep easily and slept about one-and-a-half hours longer than my usual period. I believe that this longer sleep period is what is best for me—if only I could achieve it during normal work time as well! I compromised by adding an extra forty-five minutes to my sleep cycle and feel much better because of it.

Rules For Better Sleep

Since the quality of sleep is as important as its duration, attention should be given to *every* aspect of the sleeping environment. A comfortable bed, quiet environment, and adequate time for sleep are three absolute essentials. Attention to the following simple rules will further improve your sleep:

Rule 1: Go to bed and get up at the same time every day, weekends included. A regular sleep routine builds a healthy habit and conditions the body's natural internal clocks.

Rule 2: Do not do work, read novels, or watch TV late at night if these cause your adrenalin system to become aroused. If you can only fall asleep while reading or watching TV, you've got a problem; you've conditioned your body to a bad habit.

Rule 3: As early in the evening as possible, reduce the level of illumination by turning down lights and providing a darkened environment. Darkness starts the production of an important brain hormone called "melatonin." While its precise function is not understood, it is thought to serve as a messenger to the rest of the body telling that darkness has arrived. This helps to bring down the level of adrenalin.

Rule 4: Avoid alcohol, caffeine, chocolate, spicy or greasy foods (or large amounts of any food), and cigarettes in the evening and especially near bedtime—although a glass of milk or a light carbohydrate snack may be helpful. People who drink or smoke often remain awake in bed a long time afterwards. Partly this is because they are more tense and adrenally aroused than others (which is why they need the drink or smoke in the first place), but also because of the effects these chemicals have on the body. Even though alcohol is commonly thought to make us sleepy, it actually interferes with sleep patterns.

Rule 5: Do not force sleep on yourself. Falling asleep is as natural as falling off a log if we first lower your adrenalin arousal and only do soothing, nonstimulating activities in the late evening. Forcing sleep on ourselves only frustrates us further and can cause more adrenalin to be secreted—reducing the likelihood that we'll *ever* get to sleep.

Rule 6: Find a quiet place for your sleep. If you live in a noisy environment, invest in earplugs. They are easy to get used to and effectively shut out a lot of noise. We sleep deeper and more peacefully if our brains don't have to block out background noises.

Rule 7: Exercise regularly, but do not engage in competitive or strenuous exercise just before you go to bed. Again, very rigorous exercise only raises adrenalin levels. People who exercise often sleep better because the exercise helps to use up surplus adrenalin, release muscular tension, ventilate their lungs, and create a physical fatigue that helps the onset of sleep.

Rule 8: Learn a relaxation technique such as the ones I describe in chapter 12 of this book. You can combine it with a spiritual exercise or prayer if you like. Deep muscle relaxation will help prepare you for sleep.

Rule 9: Untrouble your mind. By prayer, faith, and an attitude of trust, learn the value of "casting all your care upon him; for he careth for you" (1 Pet. 5:7). Force your mind away from problems; if you must think, divert your thoughts to less troublesome matters. A technique for "thought redirecting" is described in my book, *The Success Factor.*[1]

Rule 10: If you wake up during the night, don't get up unless you absolutely must. Relax and enjoy your light sleep. Revel in the luxury of just lying there. If you get up, read a book, or watch TV, you will push your adrenalin level back up and will have difficulty getting back to sleep again.

This is what causes many to call themselves "night people." They've caused their natural body clock to be shifted round a little. Most of them—if they so choose—can gradually shift their body clocks back to a more usual cycle by going to bed at an appropriate time and learning how to relax and enjoy sleep. Some, for practical reasons, will choose not to.

---

1. (Englewood Cliffs, NJ: Revell, 1984).

The Hazards of Evening and Shift Work

Many people, unfortunately, have to work in the evenings, and this can play havoc with their sleeping habits if they don't achieve a "shifted" body clock according to the new sleeping time. Ministers must attend evening meetings, doctors must work late at the hospital, and clerks and stockers and waitresses must work evening shifts. For them, sleep will be a challenge. Not only does night work temporarily upset the body's internal clock; but it usually takes between two and four hours after the end of the work period for the adrenalin level to drop low enough for sleep to come on. This means that if you have a committee meeting until ten in the evening it may be between midnight and two in the morning before you can fall asleep.

If you are one of these nighttime workers, what can you do about it? First of all, reduce these evening demands to a minimum. Second, if you must work nights, then adjust your waking up time by adding extra sleep time in the morning to compensate for the lost sleep. Third, if you work late only occasionally, get to bed earlier the next evening to make up for the sleep loss. Fourth, don't become frustrated if you can't get to sleep at your usual time. Allow for the extra time it takes for your adrenalin to "come down" and avoid further excitement after your work is over. Many get a "second wind" late in the evening and can't get to sleep until the early hours of the morning. This is not necessarily a healthy sign, as it could mean that their adrenalin systems are "rebounding." This can be avoided by going to bed earlier in the evening before the "second wind" has time to kick in, and by avoiding challenging or stimulating activities late at night.

If you must do "swing shift" work, then careful planning can help you prepare for the changeover period. You can start a week or two before time, gradually adjusting sleeping time to conform to the new schedule. Some extra sleep ahead of time can help your body prepare for the initial sleeplessness and fatigue that will follow the change to a new sleep schedule.

The Dangers of Sleeping Pills

Most experts agree that sleeping pills should be used only for *occasional* sleeplessness. Natural sleep is far better than induced sleep, and dependence on an artificial preparation for proper sleep on a regular basis creates havoc within the body.

A conference of experts a few years ago, assembled by the National Institute of Health, warned against sleeping pills being used for more than a month at a time. Unfortunately, there are many millions of people throughout the country who depend almost entirely on sleeping pills for their rest.

Excessive reliance on artificial sleep reduces the body's ability to return to natural sleep. It is better to try to sleep without medication and allow the body to return to its natural ways than to resort to the use of sleeping pills. While the drugs that help us to sleep are not necessarily harmful in and of themselves, they are habit-forming and make the body "lazy." One never feels really refreshed after a night of artificial sleep. Depending on the type of sleep medication used, different aspects of normal sleep will be disturbed. Some medications reduce REM sleep and disrupt dreaming, thus disturbing the organizing ability of the brain. Others increase REM sleep and reduce NREM. The changes in normal patterns of REM and NREM cut back on emotional restoration, among other things.

Happily, even for the most severe insomniac, rest and a lot of restoration can still take place in the absence of deep sleep. So long as one lies down, immobilizes the body, and gets a measure of relaxation in mind and body, the brain will replenish itself and natural sleep will return in due course. When you can't sleep, don't waste the night worrying about insomnia! Instead, enjoy the quietness and relaxation that your rest gives you. Make yourself comfortable and appreciate the privilege of a mind and heart at peace with its maker. Contemplate beautiful things, think on hopeful things, and recount the happy times of your life. And all the time you do this, your mind will be healing your body and reversing the damage that the stress of the day may have tried to work on you. If God is watching over you, your sleep can be truly restful.

"I will both lay me down in peace, and sleep; for thou, Lord, only makest me dwell in safety" (Ps. 4:8).

12

Learning to Relax

Of all the techniques available for counteracting stress and reducing the symptoms of distress, deliberate relaxation represents the most well developed and thoroughly researched. It is safe, effective—and doesn't cost anything. Not only is it the cheapest healing force we know of; it is probably the *most effective.* Believe me, relaxation is a powerful healing tool.

There are many forms of relaxation. Each system of the body has its tense or stressed state and its opposite relaxed state. The heart, when stressed, beats faster and harder. When relaxed, it ticks over at a slow and even pace. When muscles are stressed, the individual fibers are triggered into contraction more often and in larger numbers. When relaxed, the fibers stop contracting or do so very slowly, and fewer parts of the muscle are involved. Each part of the body has a stressed state and a relaxed state. My objective here is to teach you how to produce the "relaxed" state in many of the body systems at the same time.

For our purposes, I will concentrate on three areas only:
- the muscle system
- hand temperature (which represents the degree of blood flow in the hands)
- the mind.

These three systems represent the most important for counteracting the stress response. They are also the easiest to learn how to relax. Most of us could benefit beyond anything we could imagine by learning and practicing relaxation of these areas on a regular basis.

Why Relax?

Modern medicine, until recently, has neglected one of the most powerful tools for healing ulcers, headaches, high blood pressure, and stomach problems—simple relaxation. It is only in very recent years that its powerful therapeutic effects have been rediscovered.

I sincerely believe that if we could all learn effective relaxation of at least one of the major systems of the body, we could put many of the drug companies out of business. We could reduce the demand for tranquilizers, painkillers, and antacids by an unbelievable amount. We would sleep better and live longer.

This is not to deny the very real value of medication. It has its place, and I often refer patients for appropriate prescriptions of these powerful drugs. But I firmly believe that the use of drugs by themselves to treat stress—and without counseling to change the underlying cause of overstress—is patent negligence.

If you were to walk down the main street of your city and stop every person you passed, more than half of them would tell you they are taking either a painkiller, a tranquilizer, or an antacid on a regular basis. Modern medicine seems to be almost afraid of allowing us to "heal ourselves" or to let the natural healing power of the body do its own work. Any person who leaves a physician's office without at least one prescription (usually for a tranquilizer) feels as if the doctor hasn't done his or her work, and many physicians are aware of this expectation. Yet most of the same benefit can be achieved through simple relaxation in the many cases where stress is the underlying cause of the problem.

Why relax? Simply, to help the body and the mind return to their nonaroused states so that restoration can take place. Relaxing helps us "coast" when we don't need to drive hard or struggle uphill. I believe most of us try too hard to do the things that should be done easily and automatically. We live with effort instead of ease too much of the time—and this causes overstress and tension. Relaxation helps us to return to the "easy" way of living. It slows us down to the pace of life at which our body organs can recuperate and prepare us for the next set of challenges.

Relaxation also helps the body to regenerate its energy. Our overdependence on adrenalin, for instance, will eventually lead to fatigue because we burn up too much energy; this impairs our skills and dulls our minds. Restful healing allows the adrenalin system to recover and restore its ability to supply energy in large quantities when needed. If you want to reduce your distress, *YOU MUST RELAX. And you must do it often.*

Biblical Support for Relaxation

God has been calling us all along to a life of "rest." Right in the beginning, rest had a special significance for God: "And God blessed the seventh day, and sanctified it: because that in it he had rested from all his work" (Gen. 2:3).

Can you believe that? Even God "rested"!

God then instituted a special day of rest: "Six days thou shalt work, but on the seventh day thou shalt rest" (Exod. 34:21). In fact, God was so adamant about the need for this rest that he commanded the penalty for its violation to be *death* (Exod. 35:2).

Serious business, isn't it? Why? Does it not seem strange to you that God should take the matter of rest so seriously? Was he simply being arbitrary, like a neurotic parent who wants to rob his child of every bit of pleasure?

Certainly not. There is great wisdom in all God's commands. We are just too stubborn most times to understand them! But my work with stress patients and my own experience of learning to relax has shown clearly that God's emphasis on rest was for our benefit.

While the Sabbath rest of one day in seven had spiritual and prophetic significance and was ultimately culminated in Jesus becoming the Lord of the Sabbath (Mark 2:28) and our Sabbath rest (Hebrews 4:3), the Sabbath also had important *physical* significance. One had to stop *all* work, even in the middle of harvest, when time was a critical factor in ensuring that crops were gathered before spoiling. If you didn't set aside food and wood for the Sabbath day, you would starve and freeze! You could *hardly do anything* on the Sabbath except gather and worship; it was a very strict festival.

And God knew what he was doing. He knew people need rest from labor; they need relief for their knotted-up muscles, constricted abdomens, and clenched jaws. The body was never designed for continuous use, but for times of hard work alternating with periods of relaxation. Adequate time for rest was to be allowed between times of arousal. Today, our "overuse" problems are less physical than they are mental and emotional and spiritual; it is more than our bodies that need rest. We have minds that are overcluttered, feelings that are overpowering, and thoughts that are overwhelming. We need rest for them too.

Sabbaths are not to be the only resting times, either. When God gave laws, he often only stipulated the "minimum" requirement.

Jesus, faced with the hostility of Herod and the pressure of the public clamoring for healing, realized that he and the disciples were worn out; they could take no more. So he said to his disciples: "Come ye yourselves apart into a desert place, and rest a while" (Mark 6:31).

What, *rest?* With so much to do, so many sick to heal, so many souls to save? Our Type-A thought and patterns tend to balk at the idea of stopping at such a critical moment. But Jesus knew what he was doing. He knew that rest is as much a part of God's calling as rushing, and peace is as much his will as pressure. Just as surely as we are called away from our frantic, futile attempts to save ourselves, we are also called away from our hurried and hassled personalities.

When to Relax?

Relaxation should be an hourly, daily, and weekly event. *Hourly,* we should be checking up on our tensions and saying "relax" to ourselves. I would suggest placing a small, colored piece of paper or some other kind of mark on your mirror, watch dial, steering wheel, pen, or glasses to remind you to do this. Perform one or more of the relaxation exercises described later in the chapter as often as possible until it becomes a habit with you.

Daily, you should spend at least thirty minutes in deep relaxation. This is such a small part of the day that everyone can afford it—and none of us can afford not to. The best time is when you come home from work or when your early evening duties are completed. Parents of small children may find the best time is right after the children are put to bed.

Weekly, there needs to be a longer period of relaxation. Sundays or Sabbaths are ideal. On these days, cut back on work activities. Take time to put your feet up, have a nap, or just be lazy.

Much Christian church activity is unfortunately geared to make us even busier on Sundays, and I believe this can be a pitfall. If you are not slowing down significantly on your day of rest, you are going against God's intent, as well as courting stress damage.

So many of us have been raised to feel guilty about being idle for even a few minutes. But for the sake of health— spiritual, emotional, mental, and physical—we must stop our compulsive activity seeking and force ourselves if necessary into inactivity, saying, *"This is God's plan for my life. This is his call to me to rest."*

Dangers of Eastern Meditation

Before describing the techniques I advocate for relaxation, allow me to comment on some of the well-publicized meditational techniques such as yoga and transcendental meditation, since these are not the practices I will be advocating.

Many Christians are afraid that any form of relaxation may be opening the door on some pagan religious practices. Some even believe that if your mind is allowed to be "blank" for a while, evil will enter and take over.

I strongly believe this is erroneous. What sort of God would allow this? Is the solution to keep your mind so crammed full of activity that you crowd out evil? We can fill our minds with pure and holy thoughts and be at peace when we are relaxing. If we then quieten our minds, there is no more likelihood of evil's taking over than there is of Satan's rushing into our hearts just because we aren't praying. In this time of preoccupation with evil and fear of Satan, we need to remind ourselves that we are on the victory side. There is no room for a spirit of fear when we have faith. Jesus was very clear on this point when he said, "These things I have spoken unto you, that in me ye might have peace. In the world ye shall have tribulation: but be of good cheer; I have overcome the world" (John 16:33).

Transcendental meditation (popularly known as TM), yoga, and other such practices once showed phenomenal growth in the United States. They were most widely publicized in the late 1960s, but are still very much around. One of the leaders of the TM movement, Maharishi Mahesh Yogi, claims to have personally trained more than 4,400 instructors and claimed at one time to have more than a half million devotees worldwide. A movement with such phenomenal growth was bound to have some effect on the Christian church, and there has been a natural concern among Christian leaders about the impact of TM on Christians. This concern includes the impact on our Christian understanding of the nature of personhood as well as the inroads TM has made on church members, although the threat that it once posed is now diminishing. As a result, numerous books and articles have appeared challenging the claims of TM and drawing attention to its subtle evangelizing of Hindu thought and practice.

I share the concern that these Eastern religious practices are not healthy for Christians and should be avoided. My reasons for concern, however, may be a little different than those of most church leaders.

I am convinced that the claims of movements like TM or yoga to "higher" levels of effective living are grossly exaggerated. But what concerns me most is that they embellish their practices with quasi-religious frills while capitalizing on a very normal response of the body—namely simple relaxation. In other words, TM is nothing more than relaxation of the body and mind—*and God has given that benefit to all of us.* It is neither exotic nor religious, but simply a matter of practical applied psychophysiology.

What is unfortunate is that we as Christians have not shown the world as clearly as we ought that the practice of genuine Christianity can more effectively reduce stress and help people live more fulfilling lives. We are often so frantic in living out our faith that we cause more stress than we cure. This should become a challenge for us, particularly as we develop our prayer lives and rediscover that there is a Christian meditation—too long neglected by twentieth-century Christians—that can produce profound peace and communication with God. Perhaps we will then be able to share the experience of the psalmist, who said, "Mark this well: The Lord has set apart the redeemed for himself. Therefore he will listen to me and answer when I call to him. Stand before the Lord in awe, and do not sin against him. Lie quietly upon your bed in silent meditation" Psalm 4:3–4 (LB).

Basic Ingredients of All Relaxation

There is nothing mysterious or mystical about relaxation. It is a natural response of the body and can be triggered by all of us. In and of itself it does not have spiritual significance, but as we shall see it can be combined with prayer and Christian meditation to produce a powerful spiritual exercise. It is something that becomes easier as you practice it.

Whatever body system you are trying to relax, the following are the basic steps to relaxation:

(1) *Sit or lie in a comfortable position.* Pain or pressure

will keep you in an aroused state, so try to minimize discomfort. Loosen tight clothing and remove your glasses. Try to provide support for *all* the undersides of your body.

(2) *Ensure you won't be interrupted.* Lock the door; hang out a sign; tell spouse, kids, and neighbors not to disturb you, or go where they can't find you. Unplug the telephone and make sure the stove is off.

(3) *Set aside a predetermined amount of time* (say, thirty or forty-five minutes) for the exercise. Set an alarm so you won't have to keep checking up on the time.

(4) *Don't fall asleep.* If you need sleep, go ahead and sleep, but don't confuse this with "relaxing." Relaxation is a *conscious* experience, not a trance or sleeplike state. If you fall asleep when relaxing, you probably *need* more sleep. It might be a good idea to go back and read chapter 11.

(5) *Remain inactive.* Don't fidget, move, get up, or scratch. At first you'll want to do all this because you will be experiencing withdrawal symptoms from the effect of lowering your adrenalin, just as occurs when you stop taking a powerful drug. Just put up with the discomfort and it will pass away. (If the need to scratch becomes unbearable, then go ahead, but return as quickly as possible to the relaxed position.)

(6) *Avoid thinking troublesome thoughts.* Set aside your worries. Pray and "let him have all your worries and cares, for he is always thinking about you and watching everything that concerns you" (1 Pet. 5:7, LB). Try to "detach" yourself from your worrisome world for a while and remain free of the demands that press on you.

Specific Relaxation Techniques

I will now describe two more specific relaxation techniques—one for the muscles and one for hand warming. They should first be mastered independently and then tried together if desired. The techniques combine forced inactivity with visual imagery and self-talk. Together they are quite powerful to produce a deep state of relaxation.

The most effective way to practice these exercises is to

read the instructions through once so that you understand them and then to record them onto an audio cassette. Play the cassette to yourself as you go through the exercise. In this way you will become familiar with it and can implement it in other settings by recalling the instructions. And you will not have to interrupt your session by constantly peeking in a book!

If you don't have a cassette recorder, have a friend or family member read the instructions to you or read them over a number of times until you understand what it is you must do.

A TECHNIQUE FOR RELAXING MUSCLES

Make yourself comfortable. Close your eyes and shut out the world. Don't cross your arms or legs. Remove shoes and glasses. Pray and ask God to help you clear your mind of worries or resentments. Claim his peace. Now do the following:

Exercise 1: Stretching. While lying flat on your back, raise your hands above your head and rest them at the back, but don't grasp onto anything. Take a deep breath. Hold your breath for a few seconds. Relax and breathe out.

Now, stretch your hands up as far as they will go. Stretch them further. Hold them there. Now push your feet down as far as they will go. Further! Hold your arms and feet stretched out as far apart from each other as possible. Count slowly to 10: 1 . . . 2 . . . 3 . . . 4 . . . 5 . . . 6 . . . 7 . . . 8 . . . 9 . . . 10.

Relax and let hands and feet return to their original position. Again, count to 10: 1 . . . 2 . . . 3 . . . 4 . . . 5 . . . 6 . . . 7 . . . 8 . . . 9 . . . 10.

Repeat the stretching exercise once more. (If you are taping this, read the instructions again so you won't have to stop the recorder in the middle of the exercise.)

Relax. Count to five again. Take another deep breath. Hold it for a few seconds. Relax and let it go.

Repeat the whole exercise once more.

Exercise 2: Tensing. Return your arms to your side. Starting at your feet, begin methodically to first tense and relax each muscle group in your body.

First, tense the muscles of your feet and toes (without tensing any other muscles). Count to five: 1 . . . 2 . . . 3 . . . 4 . . . 5. Relax the muscles of feet and toes.

Now, move to your lower legs and knees. Tense the muscles (making sure the feet are kept relaxed). Count to five: 1 . . . 2 . . . 3 . . ·4 . . . 5. Relax and let go.

Next, the thighs. Tense them. Count to five: 1 . . . 2 . . . 3 . . . 4 . . . 5. Relax and let go.

Now, the lower-waist region. Tense all the muscles. Count to five. Relax and let go.

Now, the upper torso. Tense all muscles. Count to five. Relax and let go.

Now, the hands, arms, and shoulders. Tense all muscles. Count to five. Relax and let go.

Finally, the neck and face. Tense all muscles. (Be sure to squeeze the facial muscles as well.) Count to five. Relax and let go.

Now remain absolutely still. Don't move any muscle. Try to become aware of your entire body. Do you feel tense anywhere? Relax your jaw by dropping the lower part. If you *do* feel any tension anywhere, tense that muscle, count to five, then relax and let go. If your whole body feels tense, repeat the whole exercise from the start.

Still remain absolutely quiet. You may pray, but not about things that bother you. Repeat to yourself a verse of Scripture that helps you feel restful. I love the verse, "Thou wilt keep *him* in perfect peace, *whose* mind *is* stayed *on thee:* because he trusteth in thee" (Isa. 26:3). Or, "The peace of God, which passeth all understanding, shall keep your hearts and minds through Christ Jesus" (Phil. 4:7). Repeating verses like these will help keep out troublesome thoughts.

Breathe in and out slowly and rhythmically. Try to breathe with your abdomen, not with your chest. When you breathe in, push your stomach out and down, so that your lower abdomen expands. When you breathe out, pull your stomach in slightly.

Now remain immobile, resting and relaxing for a further twenty or thirty minutes (set an alarm or timer before you start).

When your relaxing time is over, *get up slowly*. Sit up for a short while. Move slowly and peacefully. Then go back to your normal duties.

When you have mastered the above exercise, you can try doing it while sitting. Later you'll be able to do it while driving or even working.

A TECHNIQUE FOR HAND WARMING

I have already described the importance of hand warming and explained how to use temperature dots or a thermometer for monitoring hand temperature. Review again the appropriate section of chapter 9 and make sure you have memorized the temperature values associated with each color of the dot (see figure 7).

Now, put on the temperature dot. Note the color before you start. (Or hold the thermometer between your thumb and forefinger.) Even if the temperature dot is a dark blue or violet, the warming exercise can still be beneficial.

Lie on your back, hands at your side, legs uncrossed.

Close your eyes. Relax. Let your jaw drop slightly. Take a deep breath and count to five: 1 . . . 2 . . . 3 . . . 4 . . . 5. Breathe in *slowly*. Then exhale, feeling the tension leave your body.

Now concentrate on your hands. What can you feel? A slight coldness or warmness? A slight tingling? Or do your hands feel numb and detached?

Picture yourself lying in the warm sun. Imagine that you are on a favorite beach and you can feel the sun beating down pleasurably on your hands. Hold this image. Feel the hands getting warmer. (If you don't care for the sun, make up an image of your own or try rotating through several different images.)

Imagine your hands are in warm water. The warmth comforts and heals your hands. The hands are becoming warmer as you leave them there. Feel the blood vessels of your hand becoming larger. Imagine more and more blood filling your hands. They feel like they are becoming swollen from the life-giving extra blood. They become warmer and warmer.

Say to yourself, "My hands are becoming warmer and warmer. I can feel them getting heavier and heavier." Repeat this over and over.

Remain this way for a further ten to twenty minutes, relaxing and allowing your hands to get warmer and warmer.

When you are finished, note the color of your temperature dot (or use thermometer again). If it shows a "warmer" color, you are doing the exercise right. If it doesn't, try the exercise again a little later. After some practice your hands will become noticeably warmer.

Remember, once you have warmed your hands, *remain* in this warmed condition for a period of time. The benefit comes from staying warm, not just becoming warm. You can also try the exercise sitting up.

Try Relaxation During Your Busy Day!

Take every opportunity that you can consciously to relax! When you find yourself being caught up in conflict with someone, go aside and relax if possible. When you feel a panic sensation coming over you, try relaxing. If you are worried, tense, or anticipating some troublesome encounter, use relaxation to calm your body and your mind will soon follow.

Don't expect to become a good relaxer overnight, however. Like so many other skills we learn, relaxation takes practice. Don't be disappointed if you don't succeed at first, but try and try again. Your very life may depend on it!

When you are relaxing, pay particular attention to the following parts of the body that tend to accumulate tension very easily:

(1) *The muscles of the jaw, brow, and forehead need special attention.* They tend to show your anxiety and confusion very easily. Consciously relax your brow. Drop your lower jaw. Clenching your teeth is never necessary. Whenever you have a problem to solve, remember to smooth your brow and drop your jaw.

(2) *Avoid clenching your fists or holding on to the arm of a chair or your steering wheel.* Sometimes tension creates in us a need to "hold on." It's as if we fear being thrown off our world. Consciously relax your hands, especially when holding a pen, driving your car, or watching TV.

(3) *Relax your stomach muscles.* If you pay attention, you will notice that you often tense your stomach as if to prepare for some blow in the pit of it. Too often, we live on the defensive, constantly prepared for attack. The brain receives these protective signals from the stomach and prepares the body for counterattack. But an attack almost never comes, so why not just relax? Don't *always* pull your stomach in. Forget about your posture and your figure occasionally—relax, and you'll live longer.

(4) *Watch how you breathe at all times.* There are two methods of breathing—chest breathing and belly (or diaphragm) breathing. Try not to breathe just with your chest muscles. This is nervous breathing, meant only for emergencies. It goes on high in the chest, expanding the rib cage, and it feels shallow. Use your stomach when you breathe.

Try this exercise for improved breathing: Lie on your back and place your left hand on your stomach, just below the sternum (breastbone). As you breathe in, make sure you do so by pushing up the stomach. You should see your hand rise when you do this. If it doesn't, try *pushing* it up. As you breathe out, the hand must fall. This is diaphragm breathing. It is relaxing, peaceful—the breathing style for calm people. When you breathe from your belly you can't remain tense. *Always* try to breathe this way. It could preserve your life!

13

Changing Your Type-A Behavior

If you are a Type-B person, you may wish to skip this chapter. On the other hand, you are probably married to a Type A (or work for one), so why not read it so as to understand your spouse (or boss) better!

If you are a Type-A person, it is not enough for you to learn how to relax. You must *also* change your thinking, behavior and attitudes if you are going to avoid distress and allow an even "wearing out" of all parts of your body. You can get the most out of every day of your life if you learn to be more balanced in your personality.

But kicking old stress habits isn't easy. It's harder than giving up smoking or learning to squeeze the toothpaste tube from the bottom. Years of the old patterns of thinking and behaving that lie behind your Type-A personality are not going to give up the ghost without a fight. Changing will take determination and devotion. But it's crucial to do it now. Don't wait until you are staring at the bright overhead lights of an operating room with a surgeon about to rearrange the blood vessels of your heart!

Can I Change My Personality?

Again and again, after teaching a stress management seminar and warning of the dangers of the "hurry sickness" that characterizes many of us, I am asked the question,

"Can I change my personality?"

My first response usually causes a reaction of surprise:

"No, you can't change your basic personality." But then I hasten to add the qualifier: "But you *can* change your behavior."

To me, this is wonderful news. It means that if I am a Type-A person—supercharged, superachieving, always in a hurry, impatient, intolerant—then I can learn to behave like a Type-B person—patient, tolerant, more easygoing. (Actually, you are already aware that I *am* a Type A!) If you are a Type-B person, especially if you are at the far end of the continuum where you tend to be a little too slow, never accomplishing much, then you may need to behave a little more like a Type-A person. The whole point is balance.

Our behavior, how we react to our environment and its challenges, plays an important part in determining whether and how we experience distress. Many experts believe it is far more important in causing heart disease than what we eat or inhale or how we exercise our muscles. So changing how we behave in response to stress is vital to our survival.

Recent news reports from Stanford University presented the findings of a three-year study showing that heart attack victims who received "Type-A counseling" had more than 50 percent fewer recurring heart attacks than those who were not counseled. "Type-A counseling" is simply a way of teaching Type-A people how to behave with less irritation at delays, less anger at hurts, and less aggression at competition. It also teaches them how to relax and enjoy a slower pace of life. Without this counseling and encouragement to change their behavior patterns, heart attack victims go back to creating high levels of adrenalin arousal again and merely repeat the disease process all over.

If it is true that behaving less aggressively can prevent further deterioration of the heart after the first attack, then surely behaving in a more moderate, low-adrenalin way at an earlier time in life will delay, or perhaps even stop, the decaying of the heart's blood vessels in the first place. It is never too late to change. It is also never too *early* to change.

I predict that in the next decade we will see a large increase in rehabilitation and counseling clinics designed to help us overcome our Type-A qualities. Since it has been estimated that 75 percent of the large-urban population is Type A (it is about 50 percent in the general population), large numbers of people are affected and afflicted by this personality style.

Changing Your Type-A Behavior

To be the most effective I can be in communicating how an individual can change, I want to take you through a series of steps. Be sure to take each step slowly and master it before moving on. It is characteristic of Type-A people that they try to take shortcuts. But they invariably end up not getting where they want to go, because they lose their way. Quick, ready-made solutions are not possible when it comes to changing yourself. It takes time, effort, and persistence. Type Bs have this—but then, the Type-B person may have some other personal difficulty to work through. The point is healing, not comparison:

STEP 1: ACKNOWLEDGE YOUR TYPE-A TENDENCIES

It may be a symptom of the disorder itself, or it may just be an aspect of the personality, but Type-A people tend to deny the severity of their "hurry sickness." In fact, for every five people who unquestionably exhibit Type-A behavior, perhaps four will underplay the intensity of their problem.

"But I enjoy what I am doing" or "I would never get anything done if I were different" are typical excuses. And unfortunately, our success-crazed culture also tends to glorify this dangerous behavior. As a result, no one wants to admit that he or she has a problem—until the problem gets really serious.

I have seen many patients before they have had their first heart attack—Type As, experiencing insomnia or very little sleep, headaches, tension, anxieties, and the like. They don't stay in therapy; they play down the relationship between their behavior and their distress; and consequently they don't change. Some never get a second chance.

So the first step in changing your Type-A behavior is to *admit* your Type-A tendencies. Be courageous; there is really no stigma attached since so many of us are in the same stress boat together. Admitting our destructive behavior helps us become *motivated* to change. When we do, our beliefs can more readily be modified.

As reinforcement for your admission, tell someone else about it. Commit yourself to change, and then hold yourself accountable to a friend or spouse. Accountability will help you to work harder at changing your behavior.

STEP 2: CHANGE YOUR THINKING

Behavior change *begins* in the mind.

I am currently seeing a Type-A man in therapy. He doesn't object to my telling you his story because he would like others to get the message.

This man is obsessed with making money. He thinks about it, fantasizes about it, and dreams about it all the time. He blames God for stopping him from getting it, and he became deeply depressed some months ago.

Three weeks ago I challenged this man to *stop* thinking about money. "Just think about work," I suggested. "Dwell on how you love working, on how you derive satisfaction from seeing a happy customer. Forget about the by-product of that work. If you work hard, the money side will take care of itself."

I reminded him that Scripture commands us to work hard (Prov. 10:4), but it also reminds us that the love of money is the root of all evil (1 Tim. 6:10). My words struck home and he began to change his thinking. And as he focused on his work instead of money, his depression soon lifted. His most recent words to me were, "I've started loving my wife again. I never expected that to happen just because I stopped thinking about money!"

Another client recently said to me, "If I didn't think the way I do, I'd be a happier person." She's right! A lot of our problems are due to the way we think. My book, *The Success Factor,*[1] gives some pointers on "reality thinking," and I would refer you there for more direction on how to straighten out your thinking habits. For my purpose here, I want to focus on specific ways hurried thinking produces a hurried personality.

There are three ways that Type-A thinking tends to go wrong:

(1) Type As think *continuously.* Their minds never stop; they think like a concrete mixer—churning and churning and spewing out a mix of all the ingredients originally put in.

(2) Type As think *rapidly.* Their minds race ahead of their tongues. Other people can't keep pace. Type As are often finished thinking about something before others have even started!

(3) Type As think *polyphasically.* That is, they think on different tracks at the same time. They keep two or three ideas going along simultaneously. It's like thinking in duet, trio, or even in quartet—except there's no harmony, just cacophony.

The solution to this type of thinking, then is to:

(1) *Try creating periods of "nonthinking."* Try making your mind blank for a while each hour. Focus on some pretty object or peace-inducing verse of Scripture or poetry. Deliberately choose not to think about it; just reflect on it. Stare at it, hold your mind still, and say to yourself, "I will not think—just be." Do this several times each hour.

(2) *Try slowing down your thinking.* Since all thinking is in the form of a self-conversation, try speaking to yourself *very* slowly. This can control your thinking very easily. If you speak slowly and deliberately to yourself (and pay attention), you can slow your mind down.

---

1. (Englewood Cliffs, NJ: Revell, 1984).

Try it now and see how effective it is. Say to yourself, very slowly, "I . . . am . . . not . . . going . . . to . . . think . . . rapidly." Notice how, during the pauses, you can hold off other thoughts. With practice your mind becomes very calm when you speak this way to yourself.

(3) *Try thinking* (slowly of course) *about one thing at a time.* Write your other thoughts on paper to get them out of your mind and just in case you fear forgetting them. Then focus on just *one* thought at a time. With some practice this becomes quite easy also.

STEP 3: CHANGE YOUR ATTITUDES

Most Type As are trying to prove something to themselves. Perhaps they are trying to prove they are not as useless and incompetent as they believe their parents thought they were, or perhaps they are trying to prove to God they are worthy of his forgiveness. It doesn't really matter what the reason is—the behavior is the same.

Behind our attitudes are our beliefs—beliefs about our self-worth, our calling, our dangers, and our fears of failure or success. The more you know about what you believe, the better you know yourself.

Take time regularly to do a meaningful self-appraisal. Ask, "What do I believe? What do I value? What do I want? What can I give? What can I change?" Write down a page of responses to each of these questions, and then pray and ask God to show you which are sensible and which irrational, which are essential and which nonessential.

Examine carefully your ethical and moral principles. Sure, you are a Christian. But are you honest? Do you hurt others? Are you running away from your own evil? Is success all there is to your quest in life? If you were faced with a life-threatening crisis, would all you are striving for still seem important? Is there anything cluttering your everyday living that you would be better off without?

Of all the attitudes the Type-A person must challenge and

change, the most important is the attitude toward time—particularly the *sense of time urgency*. This can lead to the "urgent" becoming a tyrannical master—and you becoming its slave.

About a year ago, a colleague of mine and I were working very hard together on a project. And it seemed very important to get that job done. I remember telling him one afternoon, "We need to get it done quickly!"

That evening I stood in the emergency room of the hospital, confronted by my colleague's lifeless body. He had died that afternoon of a heart attack. And suddenly my "we need to get it done quickly" no longer had meaning. Confronting death or seeing it cut down another's life stops the clock and forces us to take a serious look at our priorities. It has a powerful way of changing our perspective. But why do we wait until we catch a glimpse of the reality of eternity before we respond with some sensible rearrangement of our time-urgency?

The sense of time-urgency is the essence of "hurry sickness." It is often irrational, compulsive, and unrecognized. Only yesterday, I needed a spare part for my car. I found myself saying, "I must stop what I am doing and go and get it *now*." I was tense, stressed, and bothered because something was waiting to be done, and I was obsessed with doing it right away. I reminded myself that the need really wasn't urgent and talked myself out of a "hurry" episode. I need to do this all the time, and my guess is that you may, too!

There are three things I have learned about God's nature that help me to change my attitude to time and to slow down. Perhaps they'll help you too:

- God is *never* in a hurry. He knows all and never needs to rush.
- God is *never* wrong. He never makes mistakes.
- God is *always* forgiving.

Why are we so harried and hassled? Why do we wish for thirty-six-hour days when God has only given us twenty-four? Why does the fierceness of our own hostility destroy us? Why must we always prove to ourselves that we are perfect? There is only one answer—because we don't rest in God and allow his attitudes to become ours.

STEP 4: CHANGE YOUR BEHAVIOR

When you have admitted your hurried tendencies and worked at changing your attitudes toward yourself and the world, then you are ready to change your behavior. Here are some guidelines:

(1) *Improve your time management.* Much hurry is caused by bad planning. For example, a few years ago I found I was always tense when I got to work. I had developed the habit of getting up rather late in the morning and not leaving enough time to complete my preparations for work. I would have to rush to the office in order to get there on time. Being "just in time" takes its toll in terms of stress. It never allows you to be leisurely, take a stroll in the garden, listen to the birds, or enjoy the slow lane on the freeway. We fight time when we don't allow enough of it for the essentials of life.

I have since changed my behavior pattern. Now I get up half an hour to forty-five minutes earlier. I take a leisurely bath instead of a shower. I have time to read the newspaper and breakfast without feeling I am choking. And I arrive at work calm and collected. Try rising a little earlier than you usually do, and see how much better you feel. If you need the extra sleep, add it on the front end—go to bed earlier.

Plan ahead. Don't be tyrannized by never having enough time and therefore always having to rush. Also, plan for time to be alone. We all need time to collect our thoughts and restore balance to our values.

Mothers can be especially stressed by all they have to do. Mothers who work outside the home tend to be even more stressed, especially when they don't receive much help from husbands. If you are in this situation, it is especially important that you plan ahead. Make allowance for everyone else delaying you, so start your chores well ahead of time. Use a work schedule if it will help you (perhaps it will impress your husband with how much you really do). Show what must be done and when. A little extra effort here will avoid those frantic, angry, nerve-destroying rushes when you are running out of time. (You might also try *asking* for help; perhaps others in the family are not aware of how frantic you feel.)

(2) *Slow down.* If you can plan ahead how you will use your time, then you should be able to find time to slow down. But even if you can't plan for it, *slow down anyway.* I don't mean become lazy, and I certainly don't mean you mustn't care about time. But it is a fact that most of us would be more efficient and effective if we did things a little more slowly. Our quick, impulsive way of tackling tasks often means we make mistakes, and the task takes longer in the long run.

One of my bad habits as a Type-A person is that I usually believe I can carry everything that needs to be carried from the car into the house in one trip. Whether it is groceries from the supermarket, work projects from my office, or tools after I have done a repair, I believe I can save time by carrying it all in one trip. I pile my arms high, hang bits over my shoulder, and thread separate fingers into different slots— all to save time by only having to make one trip.

I have never made it yet! I always drop something and it takes me much longer than if I had simply decided to make two or three trips. After all, it's only about ten paces from where I park my car to the front door!

Lately, I have tried deliberately to take two trips when I think I can do it in one, or four if I think it is a "two-er." The result is that I feel more peaceful. I view the extra walk as exercise and use it to unwind and enjoy the garden.

I try to take *every* opportunity I can to do things the long way, so as to retrain myself into not being so hurried. And I am beginning to really enjoy slowing down. I choose the slow lane on the freeway, the slow line in the supermarket, and the slow movie on TV. Of course, I am compensating for my hurriedness by going to the other extreme, and you may not need to be so extreme. Perhaps by *forcing* myself to slow down I might just achieve enough balance so that in the future I can learn to *choose* being either slow or fast—whatever is most appropriate for the situation.

I recommend the following new habits for you to practice:

- Speak more slowly and deliberately.
- Pause regularly between phrases.
- Learn to be a better listener.
- Walk more slowly.
- Don't do more than one thing at a time.
- Eat more slowly and savor your food.
- Drive more slowly.
- Do nothing for thirty minutes—*every day.*

If we slow down these behaviors, we can slow down our metabolism, reduce our need for adrenalin, and preserve the wonderful temple of the body that God has given us for our enjoyment. We will also find time for God because it is our hurriedness that keeps us preoccupied with the unimportant and keeps our minds off him.

(3) *Plan for fewer interruptions.* There are so many things that have the potential to interrupt us and keep us from developing a peaceful spirit. The telephone, kids, neighbors' dogs, salesmen—and even the postman. Not all these interruptions are necessary, and most of them put us on edge and irritate us. The resulting anger can often aggravate our "hurry sickness" and send us into an "emergency" mode of existence.

When I first started practicing as a clinical psychologist, clients had access to my home telephone number for emergencies. It didn't take me long to become so conditioned to the ring of the telephone bell that I would jump whenever it rang. I started to hate the telephone; I would have nightmares about telephones ringing. The clanging of any bell sent me into a cold sweat! The intrusion became intolerable, especially since most of the calls weren't emergencies at all.

I resolved the problem by changing to an answering service

and having all calls screened. Most homes, I believe, could become more peaceful if they at least used an answering machine or simply unplugged the phone during important family times like meals or devotions. (I sometimes find myself wishing Alexander Graham Bell had not invented the telephone; it has become such an intrusively destructive instrument in the hands of those who do not have the courage to control it.)

Deal with other interruptions similarly. If you want time to yourself in the bedroom, hang out a sign saying "Do Not Disturb." If you want peace from noisy teenagers, take a walk in the park—and don't tell anyone *which* park.

Control your interruptions; don't let them control you. Refuse to answer the doorbell if you're busy (it's probably only a salesman). Let the telephone ring; you don't have to answer it every time. And be very clear in telling your family, fellow workers, employees, or the gardener that you don't want to be interrupted. If you can do this, you can train your mind, body, and soul to become peaceful.

(4) *Learn to laugh!* Type-A people hang onto the world as if their very life depended on it. They tend to take life too seriously, to believe they are indispensable and the world cannot function without them. They have trouble laughing at themselves. Some Type Bs are not exactly free of these problems, either.

Now, I am not advocating a denial of reality—far from it. There are certainly times when life's crises must be taken seriously, when it isn't time to laugh but to cry. But how often is life really *that* serious? So your tire is flat—laugh! So the milk has boiled over—laugh! So the dog has chewed up your favorite slippers—laugh!

Try reacting to irritations by laughing at them. The power of humor to keep adrenalin low is quite remarkable. It is very hard to live in an "emergency mode" while you are seeing the funny side of things.

My two-year-old grandson, Vincent, reminded me of that just the other day. I was teaching him how to play with a toy I had bought him. It is an airplane that flies at the end of a thin cable, operated by a battery-driven motor held in the hand. We got it to work a few times, and he was enthralled. It flew round and round above his head as he dizzily turned with the cable.

Then it crashed, and I thought the world was going to end. I was disappointed beyond words. We stood there, Vincent and I, looking at the several pieces of a once-magnificent flying machine, now scattered over the lawn. My brow was furrowed; my face was sad. He looked at the pieces, then at me, then back at the pieces—and started to laugh uproariously. My reaction to the "catastrophe" was apparently the funniest thing he had ever seen.

Then I started to laugh too, picked up the pieces, repaired the airplane and we were once again in the flying business. Vincent's child-perspective helped me to put things back in perspective.

Laughter heals anger. Laughter creates love. Laughter restores our perspective on all of life. Laughter creates cheerfulness. And Proverbs 17:22 is so very true: "A cheerful heart does good like medicine, but a broken spirit makes one sick" (LB). This is especially true when our cheerfulness is in the Lord our God.

(5) *Pray and ask God to slow you down.* Prayerlessness must surely be as great as any sin. Not to be waiting on God in the midst of our busy lives is to have no rudder, no dependable means of steering the best course. Read the Psalms and note how often we are told to "wait upon God." Psalm 25:5 says "On thee do I wait all the day." Psalm 27:14, 62:5, and 123:2 all encourage us to wait *patiently* on God.

We can so easily outrun him—to our detriment. We act before he tells us to; we react before we know his will; and we impulsively believe that he is like us in our need for haste.

Is it any wonder that we make so many mistakes in life? We choose the wrong careers; we marry the wrong partners; we move to the wrong cities; and we join the wrong churches!

And these mistakes are caused almost every time by our need for haste. And then we just as frantically try to rectify the problem, in our haste creating a second round of mistakes.

How much better to wait upon God, to move at his pace, proceed on his plan for your life—and stop making the mistakes that cause you so much distress. Jesus demonstrated a wonderfully balanced life timed to every will of the Father— never too early, never too late. He never wasted time, yet had inward rest and knew when to quit. Even though he was fully human, he also knew how to discern his Father's will day by day through a life of prayer. He knew what direction he was heading, set a steady pace, and never outran the Father. Oh, that we could accomplish God's will for us with the same beauty and composure!

14

Creativity and Stress

What makes some people more creative than others? Why are some able to be imaginative and innovative while the rest of us struggle along in the same old ruts? Are creative people born that way, or do they learn to be creative? Does it take a lot of intelligence or hard work, or is it just luck?

For a long time I've been curious about the whole process of creative thought. I've watched a friend produce whole stanzas of poetry while I struggle to find a word to rhyme with "success." I've observed others jot down the outline for a brilliant speech on the back of a napkin while I soak up spilled coffee with mine.

"What have they got that I haven't?" I've wondered. "Is it a special gift God gave just to them, or can anyone learn to be more creative?" (Not that I want to be a Mozart or an Einstein; I just want to be the best that I can be!)

Because of this ongoing fascination with the creative mind, over the years I have carried out a kind of informal study of creativity. And in the process I have learned some interesting things about creativity and about myself.

One good thing I have learned is that anybody—myself included—can learn to be more creative. I have learned that I personally seem to be most creative in the dozy early hours of the morning. And another thing I have learned is that there is a direct relationship between creativity and adrenalin arousal. Simply put, when we are most stressed, we are least creative.

This chapter will, therefore, be devoted to an examination

of how each of us can become more creative by learning new ways of thinking and by managing our stress to provide the optimal mental conditions for creative thought.

You Can Be Creative!

As a psychologist I have studied many aspects of human behavior. While much is known about how we think, there is still a lot of mystery surrounding the secrets of how some can turn on and sustain creative inspiration and others can't. We know enough, however, to say to the many who have almost given up that creativity is something we *all* can experience.

This is not to say that anyone can be a genius if he or she so chooses. There are certain levels of invention that do seem to be reserved for just a few. But all of us can learn to open the creative doors a little wider and come up with new ideas. We can do this in part by getting rid of negative and restrictive thinking habits that hinder the flow of creativity. But more importantly, we can become more spontaneous, inventive, and imaginative simply by learning to use the correct part of our brain—the "right" side in both meanings of the word. (We will discuss this in more detail later in the chapter.)

Who needs to be more creative? I think we all do—some perhaps more than others. Ministers who must prepare interesting sermons weekly, teachers who must instruct while maintaining interest and discipline, students who must complete projects or write papers, homemakers who must make meager budgets stretch to create warm and inviting home environments, engineers who must devise newer and more efficient ways to design bridges and dams—all need to be creative.

Creativity makes life more interesting and fulfilling. I believe it also places us in a more receptive frame of mind when communicating with God, since the same "unlocking" of our full mental capacities that underlies truly creative thought can also help us be more sensitive and receptive to the promptings of God's spirit. Even the hearing and receiving of God's word needs the same preparation of mind as it takes to think creatively.

What is Creativity?

Creativity is the ability to do something differently or to bring something new into being. Creative thinking is a *special* form of thinking. We are *all* capable of it within certain limits, although it is to be expected that some will be a little more creative than others.

Creativity is a normal human capacity and everyone possesses the potential for more of it. From personal experience I know that it *can* be cultivated and encouraged in *all* of us. The best analogy of the process I can think of is that of a garden. The mind is the garden that can be tilled, prepared, and cultivated, and then one can reap the benefits of one's labors. Creative thinking is a *reaping* of what one has *sown.* There can be no creative reaping if there has been no preparation of the mind's soil. As we shall see, creativity is the outflow of good preparation and of being in the right frame of mind.

What is so special about creative thought?

- *It is novel.* It is a thought or thoughts that you haven't realized before. It gives pleasure to yourself and others because it is a new way of thinking about something.
- *It is useful.* There is always some value in creativity. It helps us to learn better or to solve problems—even personal problems—more efficiently. Or it can make us more sensitive to the beauty of the world around us.
- *It is synthetic.* It helps us combine separate ideas into meaningful "wholes." We gain better perspective on life when we can see the larger picture.
- It is *solution-oriented.* When we think creatively, we come to a point of closure; we get resolution; we see

the answers more clearly to complex personal, spiritual, or other kinds of questions.
- It is *beautiful.* It thrills and satisfies and gives life a rosy edge.

Blocks to Creativity

There are many "blocks" that can get in the way of the development and use of our creative abilities. By understanding and working to remove these blocks, we can enhance our creative functioning. Here are some of the common blocks to creative thinking:
- *A fear of making mistakes.* This inhibits new learning by reducing risk taking. Creative people realize mistakes are inevitable and so know how to benefit from these mistakes.
- *Self-doubt.* This creates a negative mindset that prevents spontaneous and innovative actions. Creative people must have a fundamental belief in themselves.
- *Fear of the unknown.* Most noncreative people do not want to leave the safety of established ruts. They prefer the shelter of the known to the challenge of the unknown. Creative people, on the other hand, must be willing to engage the uncertain—at least in certain areas.
- *Taking things too seriously.* Overseriousness usually goes hand in hand with perfectionism. Together, the two attitudes tend to block creativity by emphasizing the need to be perfect and exaggerating the fear of failing. Creative people must have the courage to be imperfect and the humor to laugh at themselves and at the catastrophes in their lives.

Removing some of these blocks can help to enhance your creativity, but this is not the whole story. Creativity is also a state of mind—a special way of thinking. And many of us have actually had that way of thinking almost "trained out of us" by our culture.

A Split Brain

Some researchers have tried to explain creative thinking by seeing it as a function of the right hemisphere of the brain, rather than the left. They point out that the brain is actually made up of two separate and identical half-brains or hemispheres—a left half and a right half. The *left* half controls speech, language, logic, and reasoning. It is the "rational" half of the mind and it is the part that is most reinforced in our culture.

The *right* half, on the other hand, controls intuitive thinking, which is the basis of most creative thought. And we are not trained in the Western world on how to use this side of our brains. In fact, our educational system very much works against it!

Actually we need our whole brain to function at maximum capacity, but one or the other hemisphere tends to predominate at a given time. (Each of the two halves is capable of functioning more or less on its own.) Our Western civilization has traditionally tended to value logic and rationality over intuitive thinking, and these are "left-brain" functions. Unfortunately too much emphasis on left-brain activities can suppress the right brain with its capacity for fantasy and innovative activity—leaving us relatively noncreative and unimaginative.

How can we free up the more creative right brain? The ideas that have been suggested by educational researchers are very similar to the techniques I will describe in this chapter for giving creativity more freedom within us—although to my knowledge no one has yet endeavored to show the connection I will try to show between low-levels of adrenalin arousal and creative thinking. Researchers talk of "creative inspiration" occurring during periods of being "unfocused" and in a state of "no demand." I think there is much truth to this. Whether this state is caused by right-brain dominance or not cannot be absolutely corroborated, but this is of little consequence. All we really need to know at this point is that good stress management also enhances creative thinking.

Stress and Creative Thinking

What does creativity have to do with stress and adrenalin arousal? A lot—but not in the way we usually think.

Many of us have an erroneous belief that we are *most* creative at *high* levels of adrenalin arousal. But this is not so! In fact, a state of stress is almost certainly going to suppress any creativity.

The connection between stress and creativity is well illustrated in one group of patients. In my psychotherapy practice I see many ministers. In their preaching and teaching roles, ministers must be creative all the time. They must devise interesting sermon outlines, invent (or creatively "adapt") fascinating illustrations, and all the time be true to the Word they preach. They must hold attention yet communicate truth—and all within a twenty- or thirty-minute sermon, because the human mind has such a short attention span.

Most ministers find sermon preparation to be hard, tedious work. Invariably when I ask them when and how they set about their preparation, I discover it is usually during high levels of adrenalin arousal. They think they must "get themselves going" or "psych themselves up" before they feel they can be creative. But they are actually making it harder on themselves, because creative thought actually occurs best at *low arousal!*

General adrenalin arousal can be seen as falling into three levels:

(1) *Low arousal.* In this state, the mind is awake but not "in gear"; it is idling like a well-tuned engine without consuming high levels of energy. The mind is "unfocused" in a way that taps into *all* of its memory and resources; it can digest thoughts and engage freely in uninhibited, free-flowing thought. Low arousal is the state of reverie and daydreaming; it is in this state that memory recall and intuitive thinking are enhanced. This is the state of *maximum creativity.*

(2) *Medium arousal.* At medium arousal, the mind is wide awake and active. The body is adequately aroused and excited and prepared for moderate action. In this state one can concentrate and not be distracted, but there is no anxiety; planning is efficient at this stage, as is calculating and reasoning. Medium arousal is the stage of *maximum receptivity to information and ideas.*

(3) *High arousal.* At this stage, the mind is in high gear; it is overly alert and reactive. Adrenalin flows strongly, and there is a physical restlessness prompting one to action. At high arousal, decisions are made rapidly and action responses are almost purely reflexive. The mind is highly focused, especially on the problem or demand facing it right then, but memory recall is slow and difficult because the immediate task demands attention. This stage of arousal borders on and may even include the "fight or flight" response; at the next level of arousal there would be panic. High arousal is the stage of efficient *action.*

As we move along this continuum from low arousal through medium to high arousal, we see that the mind and body moves from a state of unfocused attention to one which is highly focused, from good memory recall at low arousal to low recall at high arousal, and from creative preparedness to "fight or flight preparedness." At low arousal, adrenalin discharge is minimal. At high arousal it is maximal.

There is also a change in the brain's electrical activity as we move from low to high arousal. At low arousal, the brain waves are slow, bordering on drowsiness; they are called "theta" waves. At medium arousal, the brain waves are typical of wakefulness and are called "alpha" waves. At high arousal, the brain waves become faster and attention is highly focused. High arousal brain waves are called "beta" waves.

The less aroused one is, the greater the number of theta waves. The more aroused you become, the greater the alpha and then beta waves and the fewer the theta waves. This understanding of how the electrical activity of the brain fluctuates with the level of arousal has led to the development of biofeedback techniques for training people to produce theta waves, which are considered to be the basis for creative thinking. We can all learn to utilize this state of low arousal without the use of expensive biofeedback equipment, however, and teaching you how is the purpose of this chapter.

Low Arousal and Creativity

There is now abundant evidence that our most inventive and creative state is at *low* levels of arousal. Contrary to what many people believe, it is when we are minimally aroused by adrenalin that we can do our most innovative and imaginative thinking.

In psychology there is a principle known as the "Yerkes-Dodson Law" (named after those who first formulated it), which states that there is an "inverted-U" relationship between arousal of the mind and body and the efficiency with which we can perform certain tasks. The law goes like this:

(1) At low arousal, we are not very effective in action tasks but very good at thinking creatively.

(2) As arousal increases, we become more effective in action and less effective in creative thinking.

(3) As arousal becomes very high, our efficiency in both action and thinking drops off again. This is probably the stage of "panic."

High arousal forces people to move away from creative and innovative responses because in the emergency they are forced back to old, familiar ways of doing things. They tend to panic and act on the reflexes instead of thinking through the alternatives.

Of course, when we have created our ideas or solved our problems at low levels of arousal, we must be able to move to a higher level of arousal to put our thoughts into action. In a sense, therefore, we need both low and medium levels of arousal for effective living. Seldom do we need a very high level of arousal in modern day living.

Let me help you recall moments when you have experienced creative thinking at low levels of arousal, so you can understand how it works.

Have you ever struggled to recall a name? Perhaps during a conversation with a friend you reminisced about old times and mentioned "old so-and-so," then couldn't recall his name? Or when cleaning out a cupboard, you placed a golf club or gadget in some special place and later couldn't remember where you had placed it? You struggled hard to force the memory back into consciousness, but to no avail; your memory for the name or place eluded you. And the harder you struggled, the more elusive the thing you were trying to recall became.

Finally you just gave up and forgot about it. You went to bed, and while starting to get drowsy you suddenly remembered the name of your old friend or the place where you hid the club! Perhaps it wasn't until the early hours of the next morning when the "aha" came to you. But it was in the unguarded, low-aroused state that the memory came back to you.

What happened? By becoming drowsy you fell into a state of *low arousal*. You triggered some "theta" waves, and in this state you unlocked the full power of your memory. Your thoughts were relatively unfocused, and this opened the doors to brain cells which at high levels of arousal were cut off because the brain was concentrating on more basic things. "Inhibitory circuits" are removed at low arousal.

I have solved many problems just when falling asleep or waking up—times when I pass through low arousal. My research work often requires that I write a computer program. Many evenings I have struggled to get a program to "run" but couldn't find the bug in it. Finally, when I've resigned myself to not being able to solve the problem, I've decided to "sleep on it." Sure as rain, I've woken up early the next morning with the error staring me in the face. As I have relaxed and allowed my mind to open up to alternative possibilities, it has presented me with the solution to my error without any struggle. This is creative thinking.

Try an experiment tonight. As you lie down to go to sleep, prompt your mind to help you recall early events from your life—events you have long since forgotten. Start by reminding yourself of some incident you can recall that occurred when you were five or six years old. Then wait. Soon your memory will present you with another incident, then another—events that you haven't remembered for years.

It is remarkable what we can recall when we are in a state of low arousal. Often in my therapy with patients who have been abused in early childhood, I use this "drowsy recall" technique to help them uncover and deal with unpleasant early experiences they have "buried" for years. Such recall of early life events—whether they are traumatic or not—can be very therapeutic. Early joys as well as hurts can come to light, and even uncovering the hurts can help free us from unconscious pain.

Steps in the Creative Process

There are four steps in enhancing your creative thinking by making use of a low state of adrenalin arousal. In explaining them, I will use the analogy of the garden, because I think it beautifully illustrates the process:

(1) We must prepare the soil of the mind by *tilling* it.
(2) We must implant ideas in the mind from which creative thought can emerge by *seeding* it.
(3) We must allow the seeds in the mind to develop to fruition by giving them time to *germinate*.
(4) Finally, we must be able to glean the benefits of creative seeding by *reaping*.

Let me provide a brief explanation of how I have used these four simple steps to enhance my own creative ability. I know they work because I have taught them in therapy to people in many walks of life.

(1) *Tilling the soil of your mind.* In any garden, the most important preparation is the removal of those contaminating influences that would inhibit the growth of new plants—weeds, rocks, insects, and so on. In the garden of the creative mind, the contaminants are such things as faulty beliefs, in-

hibitory thought patterns, and preconditioned ideas.

Some of us just think too *negatively.* We've been told—and we now believe—that we can't solve problems or think of new ideas. So we never try!

Children don't start out thinking this way. They are taught it by parents who themselves have learned it from others. Children have an inherent "pipeline to creativity" that can easily be shut off if parents do not encourage it.

I dabble a little in conjuring and sleight of hand. And I have always been fascinated by the magician who can fool me into believing he's worked a miracle simply because his hand is faster than my eye. Years ago, I used to do my magic act for Sunday school parties and was able to use it very effectively in talks to children. What always puzzled me, however, was how easy it was to fool adults, but how quickly the younger members of my audience saw through my tricks. The younger the children, the more difficult it was to fool them! Adults are full of preconceived ideas that have been drummed into them, so they believe almost any of my misdirections. But young children don't have those preconceived notions, so they see things more creatively—including being able to figure out "where the bunny went."

We "till" our minds and prepare it for creative thought by undoing some of the preconceived, negative thinking patterns of the past. We must deliberately open ourselves to new ideas and avoid making assumptions based on past experiences. When faced with a problem, we will be able to solve it more creatively if we say to ourselves, "I will open my mind to new ways of looking at this." Even when we've tried to solve a dilemma a dozen times before, we continue to open our minds to new possibilities by saying, "I'm going to approach this problem with a fresh mind and perhaps I'll see a solution this time."

Creative people, you see, don't let the past deter them from new ideas. They're always willing to try and try again. They see problems as challenges to new thinking, are open-minded, force themselves to see the world differently, keep an optimistic outlook at all times, and consequently are ready to receive a creative or God-given inspiration.

While naturally creative people do all this all unconsciously, all of us can teach ourselves to be this way by consciously and repetitively reminding ourselves of the value of these attributes. This is how we "till" the mind to make it receptive to new ideas. Doing it softens our rigidity, creates an explorer's mindset, and removes the old, inhibiting, negative thought patterns.

(2) *Seeding your mind.* Creative thinking *never occurs in a vacuum.* Gardens grow because someone has planted and tended the seed.

One reason so many never feel creative is that they do not plant enough "seed" in their minds.

Creatively spiritual people are that way because they have taken the time to study Scripture and pray. Then they merely reap what they have sown.

The creative public speaker is not brilliant because he was born with an encyclopedia of ideas in his head; he has spent time cultivating his mind by reading widely in topics he knows people would want to hear about. Then he simply reaps what he has sown.

The creative musician has spent thousands of hours practicing; the creative writer has tried writing a phrase a dozen times; the creative teacher has also done her homework. They merely reap what they have sown.

Seeding the mind can take many forms. If I am preparing to write a paper for presentation at a conference, for days or even weeks ahead of time I seed my mind by *reading* as much as I can about the topic. I talk to others about it, "bouncing ideas off them" in order to clarify my own thinking. Seeding can also take the form of *thinking* or reasoning with myself about an issue. While there is a limit to how much sense you can get out of a conversation with yourself, it can be very helpful to mentally go over the different points of view you can think of.

Seeding of the mind can best take place during medium levels of arousal. You need to be alert, attentive, somewhat focused, and in a learning mode. You are *taking in,* not giving out.

The essential point is that you can only get out what you put in. This is not to say what you produce won't be your own—or won't be creative. It will, perhaps, come out in some new form, or it will be a creative extension into some new way of seeing the idea—but it has to come from *somewhere.* Perhaps you may discover an insight that is totally new and creative, but even then it will best and most easily emerge when it comes out of a mind that has been seeded with all that can be learned about the issue at hand.

Let me illustrate this "seeding" of the mind. Suppose you are a minister and you must prepare a sermon. You have chosen a topic, but you're not sure how to present your ideas in a novel way. So you begin "seeding" your mind; you read all the background material you can get your hands on early in the week. You memorize the scripture portion on which you will preach and "steep" yourself in every available resource you have at hand. When you've done this, you are ready to let your ideas germinate. This is the third step in the creative process, to which we now turn our attention.

(3) *Allowing your thoughts to germinate.* After a period in which we seed our minds by reviewing, reading, or listening to as much as we can about the issue at hand, you need to leave it alone for a while so that it can germinate. Without being aware of it, your mind will continue to digest, ponder, play with, examine, and ruminate on your seeded ideas. You may sometimes catch yourself thinking about the subject, but a lot of the germination goes on without our being consciously aware of it.

Most of us need at least one or two days for our "seeds" to germinate. And different people find different activities conducive to the germination process. I prefer to "sleep on my seeds." During the night my mind works without my knowing it, digesting material and enlarging my brain's involvement. Others like to go for a walk, paint a house, or jog. Winston Churchill used to lay bricks; Ernest Hemingway went for an early morning stroll; and Carl Jung took afternoon naps. Any form of distraction can facilitate this unconscious digestion of ideas that will lead to the next step in creativity.

The germination of ideas is best accomplished during *low* levels of arousal. This is why so many anecdotes about the creativity of some genius or other mention that person's sleeping or napping habits. Without being completely aware of what they were doing, these great minds developed the habit of creating a state of low arousal for the germination phase.

(4) *Reaping your creative thoughts.* The final step of "reaping" can only occur after properly tilling the soil, adequate seeding, and a period of germination. It is best carried out during a low to medium state of arousal. Never try to reap when you are highly aroused, because you won't be at your best. Once your system has become adrenally aroused, creative reaping becomes almost impossible.

I prefer to reap in the first hours of the day. This is when I do my best writing or creative brainstorming. I get up early, and before I bathe or even eat, I sit down with pen and paper and begin to write down my ideas. I avoid coffee or other stimulants because I know they will elevate my arousal and cut back the little creativity I have. Perhaps very creative Type-B people don't have to manage themselves like this, but I do. And, I suspect, so do many of my readers.

I do my creative work *before* beginning my other work— whether it be teaching, seeing patients, or administration— because once I get to my office and start my daily routine, I become more aroused (even very highly aroused). And while I am then very efficient and action-oriented, my real creative ability declines. I am too "wired" and restless to be contemplative. The demands and pressures of the day kill the little bit of novel thought I possess.

When Creativity Is Blocked

Everyone at times has his or her equivalent of "writer's block"—that dreaded and mysterious shutting off of creative ideas. For the teacher it may be a lack of incentive to teach; for the musician, perhaps it is a loss of memory for where the fingers must go; for the preacher it is a dark and closed heaven. The writer knows it well—you become frozen to the chair or pace the floor like a caged tiger, trying to get an idea to write down. Try as you may, nothing—I mean nothing—comes into your head. The pen lies idle, the ink dries hard, and the paper starts to yellow!

There are a number of reasons for why writers get these blocks. They are the same reasons why anyone who must be creative occasionally becomes blocked.

Sometimes the problem is simply fatigue. We need to put down pen or chalk or violin and get some sound and solid rest.

Sometimes the difficulty is overpractice. The mind balks at being pushed again.

Sometimes the level of arousal has been allowed to get too high, and we need to "back down to a state of low arousal."

Whatever the reason, it can be helpful to go back to the beginning of the creative process and start the "tilling," "seeding," and "germinating" process over again. To change the metaphor, if we have run out of creative thought, it could be that the barrel of our mind is simply empty and needs refilling.

Also, if we wait too long between germinating a set of ideas and reaping them, we can lose much of what we have sown through the process of forgetting. It will be lost before we can reap it. For instance, three months before Christmas I wanted to write an article for a Christian magazine on why people get depressed over the holiday season. I did my research and read a few other articles to "seed" my mind. I then waited to allow some germination—but unfortunately I waited too long. I was distracted so didn't get back to the project until two weeks later. Then, when I sat down and tried to write the article, nothing came!

I started, tore up the sheet, and started again. It was hopeless. I had waited too long between sowing and trying to reap, and as in the parable of the sower, the birds of time had snatched my seeds away. I had to go back to the beginning and reread the background material for the topic—reseeding my mind. Two days later, the writing was a breeze. I had sown, germinated, and reaped in timely fashion and had great pleasure in producing my own creation.

So can you—if you understand the relationship between creativity and adrenalin arousal.

15

Spiritual Antidotes
For Stress

In the final analysis, good stress management is as much a matter of faith as it is of self-discipline and gaining mastery over our bodies. Our life in God can protect us from much distress if we don't make the mistake of thinking that the Christian life is supposed to be one hectic round of activity. The gospel is a whole gospel—tailored to suit the needs of our whole being. When we entrust ourselves to the One who has made us, we can find shelter and safety from the windy, fiery, earthquaking lives that our world so easily entices us into.

A life entrusted to God and lived in faith and dependence on him can free us from restlessness, compulsiveness, and especially our drivenness and sense of time urgency. Even Type-A people can become peaceful and patient under the Spirit's guidance and control. This is God's gift to us in Christ. We are then better able to interpret the demands of a given moment and to determine how we will respond to it. And this is true mastery over our stress.

How can we discover and develop these spiritual antidotes to stress and distress? I have already mentioned one very important antidote—the importance and power of prayer. But are there other, less obvious resources we can utilize? I believe there are, so follow with me as I explore them with you.

Jesus—The Model of a Stress-Free Life

Jesus' life was a model of *calmness and peace*—the very opposite of overstress. Look at him asleep at the back of a ship in Mark 4:38. A great storm comes up, with waves beating into the ship so that it is almost full of water. And Jesus goes on sleeping! Was he oblivious of the storm? No. Was he uncaring of the lives of others? No—when the disciples woke him and asked, "Master, carest Thou not that we perish?" he not only calmed the sea but asked them, "Why are ye so fearful? How is it that ye have no faith?" (v. 40).

Surely our lack of faith must be behind most, if not all, our stress. Most of the time we just *don't* believe God is in control! If we saw our world as Jesus sees it, would we be as frantic as we are? If we loved the world as he loves it, would we be as frenzied in our quest for self-fulfillment? I believe not. But then, we are only imperfect followers who must do the best we can to emulate his life and to live in faith.

What sort of life did Jesus model for us? Jesus' life was a model of *unhurriedness.* Peter reminds us not to be ignorant of this when he tells us "that one day *is* with the Lord as a thousand years, and a thousand years as one day" (2 Pet. 3:8).

This is a reminder (if you remember the context) that God is not slow about his promised return, even though it sometimes seems that way. He is waiting, for the good reason that he doesn't want any of us to perish. All God's delays have a purpose; in fact, everything God does is purposeful. But we have difficulty understanding this because we are so different. Our mistakes cause us to repeat our actions many times, whereas God only has to do something *once.*

Jesus' life was also a model of *balanced priorities.* When Martha received Jesus into her house (Luke 10:38–42), she was so caught up with the importance of the visit that she went into quite a dither about petty things. "Where's this; where's that; what should I cook for dinner; will he think

I'm a rotten housekeeper?"—and so on—must have rushed through her mind. Finally, she blamed Jesus because her sister Mary, who was sitting at Jesus' feet, wasn't helping her get things ready for dinner. She asked the Master to reprimand Mary and lend a helping hand.

"Martha, Martha," he chided her, "thou art careful and troubled about many things; but one thing is needful; and Mary hath chosen that good part."

We're not told how Martha took these words. I like to think she calmly put down the pot she was holding, took off her apron, pulled up a pillow, and sat down. Perhaps they didn't even bother to eat that day!

Keeping Jesus' model in mind, I strongly advocate that at least once every week we should sit down with pencil and paper and go over our priorities. Imagine that you are Mary sitting at the feet of Jesus. Write down on your list (in any order) everything you've done or want to do. List your disappointments and unfulfilled dreams, your uncompleted projects and unrealized dreams.

Then prioritize your list for the next week. Ask, "What would Jesus want me to do first? What would he want me to forget? Who would he like me to forgive?" Establish clear goals so that there is purpose to your life. More important, be clear about what really matters. Put down your pots and pans and sit at Jesus' feet for a while. This will help you to deal with the waste-products of your life, to dump the unnecessary disappointments or the criticism that comes from someone who doesn't matter anyway. Transform the desert of your pain into a beautiful garden full of fruitfulness. Receive from your Master the poise of a balanced, unhurried mind that knows the will of the Father in all things—and you will begin to be free of distress.

God's Plan Is for Unfinished Business

I taught a stress management seminar to a group of ministers not too long ago. We were in retreat high in the mountains, where God's creative beauty in nature was all around us. I had shown these ministers how to be better managers of their bodies and how to avoid distress.

Conducting the worship part of the retreat was a retired clergyman. He had seen many years of service as a minister and denominational leader all around the country, and though I had never met him before, I could tell he was held in high regard.

We came to the last service of the retreat. And to my surprise this man announced that the title of his message was to be the following prayer: "I pray that you will all die before you are finished."

At first I was taken aback. *Die before we are finished?* What a horrible idea! I had been teaching these ministers how to avoid dying prematurely, and here was this retired minister telling them to ·die before they're finished!

But as he began to unfold his understanding of God's plan, his point became perfectly clear. He was not giving a prayer for an early demise; it was a prayer for a very long and fruitful life. It was a reminder that God's plan is never finished, his work never done. He reminded us that in the great roll call of heroes of the faith given to us in Hebrews 11, "all died in faith, not having received the promises" (v. 13). Abel, Enoch, Noah, Abraham, Sarah, Isaac, Jacob, Joseph, Moses, Rahab—all lived "by faith" and "died in faith" before they had seen their promises completely fulfilled. They had to take God's word for it! "And these men of faith, though they trusted God and won his approval, none of them received all that God had promised them" (v. 39, LB).

Of course, there was a reason why these people died before they were finished. God is not a kill-joy or a sadist who would rob us of final victory just for the fun of it! "For God wanted them to wait and share the even better rewards that were prepared for us" (v. 40, LB).

What makes *us* think we will finish all *we* want to do before we die? A neurotic need to prove something to ourselves? Some memory of rejection by a parent who said, "You'll never amount to anything"? Some uncomfortable inner drive to prove that we're perfect? A hope that people will respect us more if we are successful and powerful? I suspect that the more we want to finish before we die, the more likely we'll die before we're finished! Life is, unfortunately, a chain of incompletes. We never quite finish the business of adjusting to any stage of it. We often must move on to the new just before the old is fully mastered.

At first, this realization is very discomforting. No one really enjoys having his or her life in a state of incompleteness. Most of us dream of a time when all our pursuits will be crowned with success. We hope for the time when the mortgage will be paid, our education will be completed, the redecorating will be finished or the book written. If you are a Type-A person, you are probably cursed with more than a desire to see things finished; you are most likely driven by a frenzied need to see it finished *"now."* Intolerance for delays and an obsession for closure will, unfortunately, make unfinished business hard to handle. But you too will die before you're finished! You're not likely to receive all that God has promised you in this life, either; otherwise why would we need faith?

Is it realistic to think that we can learn to accept incompleteness and still be content? I think so! A successful life will *always* be unfinished, and the more successful it is the more will be left undone. This is how life works. It may seem sad, but the positive side to all of this is that God is with us in our incompleteness and gives us permission to stop trying to accomplish everything in one brief period of existence. It is liberating to realize that *we don't have to finish.* All we have to be is *faithful.*

If you want to control your stress and reduce the pain and threat of distress, remind yourself each morning, midday, afternoon, and evening that you will always have to leave something unfinished. Place a note on your dressing mirror to remind you of this. Put a marker in your bible pointing you to Hebrews 11. The "tyranny of the urgent" will be conquered if you give up on trying to run a race with death. You will then feel you have "permission" to put down that pen, pack away your paintbrushes, or leave that project until tomorrow!

Try "finishing" only that which must be finished now. Great buildings are built by laying one brick at a time. Great poems are written one word at a time. Long distances are traveled by taking first one step and then the other. Try thinking of your immediate task as simply taking one step or laying one brick. If it is correctly placed in position and cemented bottom and sides, *that task is completed.*

Everything that must be accomplished breaks down into little steps. Finish each step, take the steps one at a time, and then relish the sense of completeness. Then you'll live to be able to take the next, and the next step.

Charles E. Hummel, in a booklet entitled "Tyranny of the Urgent," [1] points out that much of our suffering is due to our jumbled priorities. He reminds us of the great prayer of John 17 in which, Jesus said, "I have finished the work which thou gavest me to do" (v. 4).

Hummel asks: How could Jesus use the word *finished* when all he had was a three-year ministry? A few found healing in him, and *some found forgiveness* and a new life, but is that an adequate basis for saying "finished"? What about the hordes who still hobbled on paralyzed legs or rotten, leprous stumps? Have you ever wondered and tried to figure out what happened to the broken people Jesus walked by and didn't heal? For every one who was touched, a hundred must have been at the back of the crowd and not even seen by him.

And here is Jesus, coming to the last night of his earthly life. All around him there is still hunger, disease, and sin, rampant and overwhelming. And what does Jesus say? "It is finished!"

The only sense we can make of this is to believe that when his earthly life was over his real work had *only begun.* Since Jesus knew the Father's greater plan of healing and salvation,

---

1. Downer's Grove, IL: Inter-Varsity Christian Fellowship, 1967.

he could resign himself to the immediate incomplete task and say, "It is finished." There was no feverish, frantic rush to do everything as quickly as possible because he could see that time was rapidly running out.

I venture to suggest that if you and I could get a glimpse of God's greater purposes, we would also be less frenzied. We would also be able to resign ourselves to dying before we're finished, because in a sense we will have finished his immediate assigned task. We would be peaceful in the presence of pain and patient in the presence of pressure. We would not panic when we see our life rapidly passing away with so much left unfinished. Our prayer would also be, "I have finished the work which thou gavest me to do" as we pass on to another person the plans we never carried out or the dreams we never accomplished.

Only God is indispensable. I am grateful to the preacher who helped me realize this through his prayer "that I die before I am finished." This prayer and the concept behind it has helped me be less tyrannized by my drive for perfection.

Coping With the Stress of Sin

You may remember from an earlier chapter that sin is a stress problem as well as a spiritual one. But the beauty of the gospel is that God has made a provision for coping with sin. If we accept this provision as he gives it to us, we can eliminate a lot of stress from sin in our lives.

Here is a brief outline of the way God helps us deal with sin in our lives:

(1) *He brings us awareness of our sin.* Mostly this comes through Scripture and the caring confrontation of others in our lives. We are told clearly in 1 John 1:8 that "If we say that we have no sin, we are only fooling ourselves" (LB).

(2) *He offers us forgiveness for our sin.* This is one of the central messages of the New Testament. All we have to do is confess our sins to him and ask for his forgiveness. "But if we confess our sins to him, he can be depended on

to forgive us and to cleanse us from every wrong" (1 John 1:9, LB).

(3) *He brings us restoration of our highest purposes.* Once we have been forgiven, we are made new. We no longer have to spend our time worrying about the sins of the past; we can turn our sights to doing what God would have us do in the future: "Christ himself can use you for his highest purposes" (2 Tim. 2:21, LB). Remember, God wants us to be the very best we can be—and that means living healthy, distress-free lives.

Spiritual Resources for Coping with People

We also saw in an earlier chapter that people are one of the prime causes of stress. But we also saw that we *need* people—and at any rate we can't avoid them. So how can we deal more effectively with people and thus keep our stress levels down? I believe the Bible holds two very important principles:

THE LOVE PRINCIPLE

Is there any principle of Christian living more emphasized by Jesus, who said, "Your strong love for each other will prove to the world that you are my disciples" (John 13:35, LB)?

The role of love in reducing stress can be quite remarkable, but many people are still unsure what it means to love. I would refer the reader to chapter 9 of my book, *Feeling Free,* [2] in which I discuss this in more depth. For our purposes here, I simply want to draw attention to three common misconceptions of love that seem to get in many people's way:

Misconception 1: "Love is a feeling." Christian love is *not* a feeling, but a set of behaviors (see 1 Cor. 13). It is how I treat another—not how I feel about him or her—that deter-

---

2. (Englewood Cliffs, NJ: Revell, 1979).

mines the extent of my love. If I am patient; kind; never jealous nor envious; not proud, selfish, or rude—*then* I am loving.

Love feelings are the *consequence*, not the *origin*, of loving acts. When I behave toward others in a loving way, I usually begin to feel love for them. But if I wait until I have the feelings before I begin to love, I may have to wait forever!

Misconception 2: "Loving is liking." Perhaps this is the most confusing idea of all. Our lives are full of people we don't enjoy, and I am so thankful that God doesn't tell us to like them—only to *love* them.

We are even commanded by Jesus to love the very people we *don't* like! "Love your enemies" is what we are told in Matthew 5:44. Obviously, if someone is our "enemy," he or she is hardly someone I will like. So we must stop letting our dislike of people get in the way of our loving. But it is possible that if we start loving people, we might *begin* to like them.

Misconception 3: "Loving is not hating." We often believe that if we hate someone, we can't possibly love them. Not so! Love and hate are not opposites. Love and *fear* are opposites. Love and *indifference* are opposites. But love and hate are two sides of the same attitude. In fact, intense hate is often a symptom of a deep love that has been rejected. If you hate, your feeling most likely comes from wanting to love deeply and finding that your love is thwarted. If we take a closer look at those we hate, we might find a hidden love. Then we can go ahead and give expression to it! Doing so will significantly reduce our stress.

THE FORGIVENESS PRINCIPLE

Love and forgiveness are closely tied in Scripture. To love is always to forgive. Not to forgive is not to love.

As I show in chapter 5 of *Feeling Free*, great freedom from anger is possible through the gift of forgiveness. I doubt if a deeply forgiving person ever suffers from severe stress disease. Think about that! Of course, anger is not the only cause of stress damage, but it certainly is a significant one. So being able to forgive the many people who cause us hurts can help keep us free of distress.

Because forgiveness is such an important spiritual principle when it comes to dealing with stress, I will discuss it more completely in the next section of this chapter. But for now, remember these important points about forgiveness:

- Forgiveness does not necessarily condone the behavior of another.
- Forgiveness leaves justice in God's hands.
- Forgiveness protects the forgiver from himself or herself.
- Forgiveness is always for the *forgiver's* benefit.
- Forgiveness does not need the other person to acknowledge what he or she has done.
- Forgiving others is the other side of being forgiven by God.

How Can We Forgive?

Forgiveness is a special gift the Bible offers us for healing our deep-seated resentments, whether the hurts we experience are deserved or not. But forgiveness isn't always easy. How do we learn to forgive when our feelings of hurt are painful and deep?

A recent patient shared with me a long list of her deep resentments. And she has had more than her fair share of life's hurts. Her birth parents abandoned her as a baby because they wanted to be "free." Her adoptive parents were cruel and abusive. An uncle raped her when she was nine. As an adolescent she developed a bad skin condition that turned her away from friends and made her feel like a misfit. Even though she is quite intelligent, she has not been able to accomplish a significant educational goal. Her first husband abandoned her for another woman. And the list goes on and on. In fact, the only positive aspect of this woman's life when she began coming to me was a faint but stubborn belief that there is a God who just might care a bit.

As you can imagine, this woman had a lot of deep-seated anger at the world, at herself, and at the God she hoped was still there. "What can I do?" she asked with tears of anguish streaming down her face.

"Let me help you discover the freeing power of the forgiveness that God makes possible," I whispered, with a few tears trickling down my own cheeks. "I think God has already prepared the way for your healing. He must have known that sooner or later someone with just the messed-up life you've experienced was going to come along," I said.

I then went on to explain that secular psychology really has *no* answer for such deep hurt and resentment for life's unreasonable, lopsided dispensing of unfair pain and suffering. Only God has the answer.

I then read her Matthew 5:38–48:

The law of Moses says, "If a man gouges out another's eye, he must pay with his own eye. If a tooth gets knocked out, knock out the tooth of the one who did it." But I say: Don't resist violence! If you are slapped on one cheek, turn the other too. If you are ordered to court, and your shirt is taken from you, give your coat too. If the military demand that you carry their gear for a mile, carry it two. Give to those who ask, and don't turn away from those who want to borrow. There is a saying, "Love your *friends* and hate your enemies." But I say: Love your *enemies!* Pray for those who *persecute* you! In that way you will be acting as true sons of your Father in heaven. For He gives His sunlight to both the evil and the good, and sends rain on the just and on the unjust too. If you love only those who love you, what good is that? Even scoundrels do that much. If you are friendly only to your friends, how are you different from anyone else? Even the heathen do that. But you are to be perfect, even as your Father in heaven is perfect (LB).

In this passage, Jesus reminds us that under the old law the rule of life was simple: If someone hurt you, you were entitled to hurt that person. An eye for an eye and a tooth for a tooth was the law of survival and punishment. But in this passage he steps beyond that old law. It never really worked anyway, because if someone took out your eye, you would not be content with just taking one of theirs—you wanted both. Psychologically, revenge is *never* fair; it always wants more. Now Jesus is saying, "If someone hurts you on the right cheek, turn the left also."

Oh, how we misunderstand Jesus and balk at his wisdom. Our lower nature wants revenge, not more hurt. Turning the other cheek seems like the act of a coward. "They'll just stomp all over me" is what most of us cry back to Jesus; "they'll get away without being punished" is our deep-seated fear.

God knows that our natural tendency is to seek revenge. He also knows that the chain of revenge never ends. If I take out your eye, then you will want to take out mine; I will then want your other eye, and you will retaliate with my second. The result: we will both be blind, and neither will be satisfied. *The cycle of revenge never ends.* This is why anger must be cut off *before* it resorts to revenge.

In Matthew 5:38–48, Jesus is saying to us that the best way to deal with our hurts is to love the ones who are doing the hurting. He calls them our "enemies." The call is for us to exercise forgiveness as the antidote for the anger at being hurt. "Cheek turning" is an act of forgiveness.

After telling us in Ephesians 4:26 that we can be angry but should not sin, Paul also goes on to tell us: "Stop being . . . angry. . . . Instead, be kind to each other, tenderhearted, forgiving one another" (Eph. 4:31–32, LB).

How? There is only one way in this world, and the passage goes on to give it: ". . . just as God has forgiven you" (v. 32).

I can forgive those who hurt me only *because* God has forgiven me for the hurts I have caused him. I forgive them because I need to protect myself from my own revenge. I forgive them because, in effect, God has said, "*I* do the punishing around here; all I want you to do is the forgiving."

I know that just saying "you must forgive" can be glib

advice when you are hurting very deeply. When does the hurting stop if your enemy just keeps on hurting you more? Obviously, there are times when we must be assertive and call a halt to unnecessary emotional or physical pain. But confrontation is a very different thing from revenge. And we will be most effective in confronting and stopping injustice and anger when we have *first* taken the step of forgiveness.

What do I do when I forgive? *I surrender my right to hurt back.* I lay down the axe just as I am about to bring it crashing down on the head of my enemy. And I do it for *one* reason only: *God has asked me to.* In return, he offers me the greatest gift anyone can know—to be at peace with the Creator of the universe and the Master of our souls. This is a more powerful stress reliever than any tranquilizer or blood pressure medicine. I know, because I've tasted it myself!

> What God can compare with you:
> taking fault away,
> pardoning crime,
> not cherishing anger forever
> but delighting in showing mercy?
> Micah 7:18 (JB)

Appendix 1

Keys to Figures 2, 4, and 5

Interpret your final "scores" for the stress tests on pages 45, 76, and 108 according to the following charts:

FIGURE 2

Total | Interpretation

0–5 You are definitely not a Type-A person. You may slip into Type-A behavior, but not often enough for it to be a problem.

6–10 You show occasional signs of Type-A behavior. You may have a temporary irritation in your life, or perhaps some aspect of your work is getting to you. You are approaching the Type-A behavior pattern as you near the upper end of this score.

11–16 You show definite signs of being a Type-A person. At the higher end of this score, you are becoming prone to excessive adrenalin recruitment and are likely to be evidencing signs of distress.

17–24 Not only are you a Type-A person; you are living dangerously! Life may be miserable for you, or it may be very exciting. Either way, you are likely to develop cardiovascular deterioration if you do not change your behavior pattern. If you smoke or have any of the other high-risk factors (diabetes, high blood pressure, or a family history of heart disease), I advise you to seek professional help as soon as possible.

FIGURE 4

Total | Interpretation

0–10 No stress. Are you sure you are alive?

11–20 Mild stress. You are basically healthy, but occasionally bothered by stressful life events.

30

21–30   Moderate stress. You should be concerned about your life
        pressures and how you handle them.

31–40   Severe stress. Your life is out of control and you probably
        need professional help.

41–60   Dangerous stress levels. You need immediate help.

FIGURE 5

Total   *Interpretation*

0   If you are sure you have been honest with yourself in
        answering the questions, you can rejoice. You have devel-
        oped a remarkably calm and serene way of looking at
        life, and your reward will be better physical and emotional
        health.

1–4   You are probably in the safe range, but the lower the
        better.

5–6   Your stress levels are moderate, but you may still need
        to change some aspect of your life to avoid suffering some
        stress damage.

7–10   You are the victim of a lot of stress. If you don't make
        some changes soon, you may find yourself the victim of
        stress disease.

Appendix 2

How to Order Temperature Dots

Temperature dots indicate stress levels by changing color to indicate surface skin temperature. They can be ordered from either of the following sources:

(1) Mindbody, Inc., the company which first developed the dots under the registered trademark Stressdots®, is an educational extension of the Wholistic Health Center and Institute for Self Development, the largest facility of their kind in the United States. In addition to Stressdots®, they offer audio cassettes with specialized relaxation exercises and "executive stress kits," which combine taped relaxation exercises with biofeedback tools. For a brochure and price list, write or call:

> Mindbody, Inc.
> 50 Maple Place
> Manhasset, NY 11030
> (516) 365–7722
> *407-495-4700*

(2) The Conscious Living Foundation, which manufactures dots under the name Stress Spots, is a nonprofit, tax-exempt foundation that specializes in research and education in stress management and biofeedback. In addition to the dots, they sell audio cassettes and a variety of biofeedback equipment. For prices and a free catalog, write or call:

> Conscious Living Foundation
> PO Box 9
> Drain, OR 97435
> (503) 836–2358

Index

ACTH hormone 37
Activating system 67, 69, 70, 71–72
Adaptability 25–26, 119
Addiction, adrenalin 14, 83–89, 93, 95, 131
Adrenal fatigue 89–93
Adrenalin management 13–14, 40, 102–3, 137, 144
Adrenalin monitoring 115–19, 134
Aggression 103, 179
Alarm system 21–23, 67, 68, 69, 70, 71–72, 112
Allergies 79
Anger 30, 40, 41, 42, 68, 70, 73, 101, 103, 109, 110, 112, 121, 139, 142–45, 179, 187, 189, 215, 217, 218, 219
Anxiety 20, 25, 51, 56, 73, 81, 84, 85, 90, 91, 96, 101, 141, 146, 151, 180
Arousal, adrenalin 12, 14, 15, 22, 24, 26, 27, 30, 34, 37, 38–39, 50, 51, 57–60, 67, 75, 81, 86, 90, 93, 94, 95, 96, 101, 115–28, 131–38, 140–41, 142, 147, 149, 151, 154, 157, 158, 160, 168, 172, 179, 191, 195, 196–206
Assertiveness 110, 142, 219
Atherosclerosis 34
Attitudes 12, 82, 86, 161, 178, 183–85, 194, 215
Backaches 26, 38, 73, 92
Beliefs 147, 152, 181, 183, 194, 196, 200
Beta-Blocker 148
Biofeedback 13, 125, 126, 127, 128, 197–98
Blocks to creativity 194, 204–6
Blood pressure 12, 25, 26, 27, 28, 34, 37, 60, 73, 90, 96, 101, 116, 119–21, 143, 147, 156, 166, 219
Breathing 28, 73, 135, 156, 174–75, 177
Burnout 61, 154, 155
Cancer 23, 80, 146
Changes 49–50, 61, 62, 63, 107, 141, 178–90
Cholesterol 12, 34, 38, 39, 40, 96–104, 127, 141
Christian meditation 171
Cluster headaches 78

Cold hands 38, 73, 78, 116, 125, 126, 134–35, 136
Competition 30, 88, 103, 179
Cortex 37, 90
Cortisol 37, 128
Cortisone 37
Creativity 11, 24, 159, 191–206
Dependency 83, 84, 85, 86, 97
Diet 99–100, 103–4, 121
Dream sleep 157–58, 163
Eastern meditation 169–71
Eating habits 23
Electromyograph 126
Energy 14, 24, 38, 39, 50, 57, 69, 73, 86, 90, 91, 92, 115, 136, 153, 167, 196
Eustress 24, 28, 50–51
Exercise 12, 40, 85, 91, 96, 99, 100–101, 103–4, 118, 138, 161
Fatigue 57, 73, 90, 92–93, 136, 153, 161, 167, 205
"Fight or flight" response 15, 22, 26, 30, 37, 67, 70, 78, 103, 106, 143, 197
Fluorescent lights 79
Forgiveness principle 215–19
Good stress 24, 50–52
Hand warming 175–76
Headaches 26, 27, 35, 38, 69, 70, 77–79, 90, 110, 143, 166, 180
Heart disease 12, 33–34, 39, 41, 67, 96–97, 98, 100, 101, 102–3, 131, 141, 151–52, 179
Heart rate 90, 116, 118–19
Helplessness 102
Hidden stressors 25, 75, 105–14
High arousal 14, 26, 27, 34, 60, 75, 81, 94, 125, 134, 147, 149, 179, 196, 197, 198, 204, 205
Hurry sickness 11, 41–49, 52–54, 56, 61, 62, 63, 128, 178, 180, 184, 187
Hypoadrenia 90
Illness 19, 23, 33, 35, 49, 57, 81, 82, 90, 106, 136, 140, 149–50
Immune system 80, 81
Laughter 188–89, 194
Left hemisphere 195
Lifestyle 19, 155

Lipoproteins 34, 97–98
Love principle 214–15
Low arousal 24, 51, 123, 132–33, 137,
    157, 195, 196, 197–98, 199–200, 204, 205
Medication 13, 35, 81–82, 87, 102, 147–
    48, 163, 166, 219
Medium arousal 37, 90, 197, 198, 202,
    204
Migraine headaches 12, 73, 77, 78, 125
Minor hassles 107
Mood rings 121
Muscle tension 26, 38, 73, 78, 92, 116,
    126–27, 134, 138, 161, 174, 176–77
Negative thinking 192, 194, 201–2
Night people 151, 155, 158, 161
Nondream sleep 157–58, 163
Pain 28, 48, 63, 64, 67, 68, 70, 71, 73,
    75, 77–78, 80–82, 86, 93, 96, 109, 110–
    11, 112, 117, 126, 145–47, 200, 209, 211,
    213, 216, 217, 219
Panic disorder 28, 73, 81, 91, 92, 147,
    148, 197, 198, 213
People as cause of stress 109–10, 112,
    214
Peripheral vasoconstriction 116, 121
Pituitary gland 37, 116
Post-adrenalin depression 71, 86, 148
Prayer 48, 57, 59–60, 100, 133, 145, 146,
    161, 171, 172, 173, 183, 189, 202, 207,
    210, 212, 213
Raynaud's Syndrome 125
Reality thinking 182
Recovery system 67, 69, 71–72, 90
Recovery time 48, 140–41
Relaxation 19, 43, 47, 50, 53, 60, 84, 89,
    103, 133, 135, 136, 137, 138–39, 142,
    146–47, 156, 161, 163, 165–77, 178

Revenge 217–18, 219
Rheumatoid arthritis 80
Right hemisphere 192, 195
Risk factors for heart disease 33–34,
    96–97
Sabbath 51, 144, 167–68, 169
Saturated fats 199
"Seeding" the mind 200, 202–3, 205–6
Self-talk 137–38, 172, 182–83
Sexual addiction 93–95
Shift work 162
Silent killer, high blood pressure as 34
Sin 95, 109, 111, 112–13, 213–14, 218
Skin temperature 60, 111, 121–26, 143
Sleep 23, 39, 68, 73, 77, 84, 85, 87, 89,
    93, 141, 142, 149–64, 185, 199, 203, 204
Sleeping pills 155, 163
Sleeplessness 92, 149, 151–52, 155, 163,
    180
Sources of stress 37, 105–14
Spiritual antidotes 144, 207–19
Spiritual energy 56–57, 93
Spirituality 55–64, 93, 111, 132
Symptoms of distress 56, 67–82, 90
Temperature dots 122–24, 175–76, 223
Tension 20, 84, 96, 110, 160, 167, 169,
    176–77, 180, 185
Tension headaches 12, 68, 77–78, 92
Time management 185–86
Time urgency 11, 44, 46, 184, 207
Tranquilizers 81, 166, 219
Type-A counseling 13, 179
Type-A personality 13, 34, 41–46, 52, 89,
    102, 125, 138, 178–90, 207, 211
Ulcers 12, 23, 27, 29, 35, 38, 92, 143, 166
Withdrawal 85, 86, 88–89, 159, 172
Workaholism 87–88